P9-EDG-813

"*The Pattern is an autobiographical account of personal transcendence. By sharing her journey with so much honesty (and humor), Lynnclaire Dennis contributes to our understanding of spiritual development. The provocative experiences described in this book, and the 'pattern' they imply, will resonate with many readers.*"

—Stanley Krippner, Ph.D., professor of psychology, Saybrook Institute, and coauthor of *Personal Mythology* and *Spiritual Dimensions of Healing*

"*Most near-death experiencers have worthwhile tales to tell, but what makes Lynnclaire Dennis's story so unusual and inspiring is what she brought back from her sojourn to the Light as a gift for all humanity—it is something that may not only change your life, it may change the world.*"

—Kenneth Ring, Ph.D., professor of psychology, University of Connecticut, and author of *The Omega Project* and *Heading Toward Omega*

"*It is my impression that* The Pattern *presents a very new and different insight into the very essence of life's structure. I consider it a most worthwhile addition to the existing literature regarding near-death experiences and their consequences, and recommend it on that account alone very highly.*"

—Hans Holzer, Ph.D., author of *The Secret of Healing, Life Beyond*, etc.

"*The Pattern of Healing is a powerful symbol, a representation of humanity's spiritual essence. The Pattern reminds me of the quiet presence at the core of all being, the peace which passes all understanding. If Lynnclaire Dennis had not experienced the Pattern directly, we would have wanted to invent it. The Pattern brings love to light; it brings new hope to the heart of our world. It is, to me, the symbol of a world reborn, a world at peace.*"

—Prof. John Gardiner, Ph.D., cofounder of The Willoughby Foundation, The Pacific Northwest Postdoctoral Institute, Seattle University

"*The Pattern suggests a static representation of the chaos theory rule: period three implies chaos. It seems likely that the information revealed to Lynnclaire is intrinsically dynamic, the chaotic dynamic being implied by the static representation of the Pattern. This would be consistent with the perception that the Chaos Revolution dawns a new epoch in our cultural evolution.*"

—Ralph H. Abraham, Ph.D., professor of mathematics, University of California at Santa Cruz

"*The Pattern (as represented in photos) is it, but it's not it—it needs to be dynamic, not static. It is staggering from a neurological perspective that Lynnclaire was able to retrieve the Pattern. This is the first time since Newton that a cultural experience will effect and redefine science and technology—Newton having been influenced by the work of Jakob Böhme, the Dutch shoemaker, philosopher, and mystic.*"

—George Mpitsos, Ph.D., neurophysicist, director of the Hatfield-Mann Science Center, Newport, Oregon

"The Pattern is a universal representation of the energy of creation. Contained within it are the symbols of all the world's spiritual traditions, calling for Oneness of heart and mind as we manifest a new world. The vibration of the Pattern is pure love, and its reemergence in this era will be a powerful catalyst to individual and planetary healing."

—Joan Borysenko, Ph.D., author of *Minding the Body, Mending the Mind*, etc.

"The Pattern evokes a response which can be a meaningful and powerful physical healing response. It appears to be open to almost infinite individual interpretations, all of which, in the considerable experience gathered to date that I am aware of, have been of a positive and supportive nature. Given what is already known about the role of symbols in healing, it is of particular importance that the potential embodied in the Pattern for mobilizing healing forces within a human being be rigorously investigated in all its facets and possible applications."

—Alan Shackelford, M.D., physician

"When I first saw the Pattern, I was very curious, but curiosity soon turned to astonishment, as I perceived sacred symbols of all spiritual traditions within this one continuous form."

—Miron Borysenko, Ph.D., psychoneuroimmunologist

"My initial response to the Pattern is that of movement and stillness and their complementary partnership with each other. What a metaphor for life (at least as I experience it). Life and the Pattern both having its open and closed aspects, its changing as well as enduring aspects. Its wave nature versus its particular nature, the fluid versus the fixed. The multiplicity of forms versus one form; so many apparently different forms yet actually one form looked at in different ways from different perspectives. What holds these different aspects of the Pattern together? My imagination says that it is love, the love of stillness for the beautiful motion and the love of motion for the stillness. Could gravity serve this same holding-together function in life as the physical analogue of Love? It keeps the solar system together and perhaps also the soular system, keeping us all on the planet and keeping us in relationship as we gravitate toward others. Love, gravity, Soul—could they be different forms of the same thing?

—Robert Goldhamer, M.D., psychiatrist

"I think that not only does the Pattern present a new way to unite the human race, but it represents the Pattern of completeness that we will somehow create with the evolution of man. The Pattern is the symbol for love. I think it and the ideas that are presented in The Celestine Prophecy will change the world. I hope I will be given a chance to join in with the spiritual evolution and lead the world into a new and brighter future."

—Julie Hackett, student, age 14

THE PATTERN

The Pattern

The Pattern

The Pattern is a hypertetrahedral, holonomic structure.

It consists of a tetrahedral tube

forming three rotated and internesting loops

that weave around a central 144-faceted, tetrahedral sphere

of approximately half the diameter of the loops.

This dynamic structure is in constant motion,

rotating on a north-south axis at 22.5 degrees,

expanding and compressing

from both the vertical and horizontal planes.

THE

The Pattern

PATTERN

LYNNCLAIRE DENNIS

Integral Publishing
in association with
Entagram Productions Inc.
1997

Copyright © 1997 by Entagram Productions Incorporated

All rights reserved. No part of this publication may be reproduced or transmitted in any form or by any means, electronic or mechanical, including photocopying, or stored in any information retrieval system, without permission in writing from Integral Publishing. Reviewers may quote brief passages.

Published by: Integral Publishing
                  P.O. Box 1030
                  Lower Lake, California 95457

In association with: Entagram Productions Inc.
                       P.O. Box 152
                       Tiburon, California 94920

The names of several individuals in this book have been changed to protect their identity. This book is a true chronicle, however, not a fictionalized account.

Readers wishing to contact the author may write to her c/o EPI, P.O. Box 152, Tiburon, CA 94920. To order additional copies of the book and other products associated with the Pattern (please see descriptions on the last two pages of this book), call toll free 1-800-575-1612. The Pattern World Wide Web site address is http://www.kitsap.net/pattern/.

Cover and text design and typesetting by Beth Hansen, Petaluma, California.

Cover art and inside color plate based on computer modeling of the Pattern by Wiseguys' Graphics, Seattle, Washington.

Line drawings by Kathleen Sohn-Foster, Sebastopol, California.

Printed in the United States of America.

03 02 01 00 99 98 97

10 9 8 7 6 5 4 3 2 1

Library of Congress Cataloging-in-Publication Data

Dennis, Lynnclaire, 1951–
    The pattern / Lynnclaire Dennis.
        p.   cm.
    ISBN 0–941255–50–6 (cloth : alk. paper)
            1. Dennis, Lynnclaire, 1951–   .   2. Spiritual biography—United States.
        3. Example—Miscellanea.   I. Title.
    BL73.D46A3   1997
    291.4'092—dc20
    [B]   96–43434
                                                                                            CIP

The paper used in this publication meets the minimum requirements of the American National Standard for Information Sciences—Permanence of Paper for Printed Library Materials, ANSI Z39.48-1984.

$\mathcal{D}$EDICATION

$\mathcal{T}$his book is in memory of my father, James Henley Dennis, who in 1987 presented me with the precious gift of choice when he shared with me the truth that I would never rediscover the Light by analyzing the darkness.

This work is also a tribute to my greatest teachers, my children.

To my daughter, Julia Alysse Haines: You are a beautiful woman who has become the most precious gift a mother could ever desire—my friend.

And to my son, Ryan Oliver Haines: You are light in an oft dark world. Your love and willingness to forgive have kept our spirits tethered over time and far too great a distance. You are my inspiration.

You spark joy in my heart,
light my world with grace,
and daily renew my belief
that there is a new day dawning
which heralds a bright promise
for future generations.

CONTENTS

$\mathcal{P}$ ATTERN

Pattern reigns supreme
To see and govern all the world
And regulate the flowing stream
Of conscious thought
And perception's dream.
It blends and fades and reappears
To form meaning from wondrous fears,
To captivate in human awe
A symmetry with not a flaw.
It turns a graceful pirouette
And cries again in places as of yet
Unheard, unseen, unthought or met.
Its cadences repeat and ring
To echo to a cosmic beat,
And find in this polyphony
The guarded source of the discrete.

$\mathcal{C}$*omment:* In this poem, the pattern itself is beyond any specific visualization, for it is the source of particularity. I think that we each have our own intuitions about this, and that for each of us certain specific patterns and forms have tremendous meaning just because they lead us beyond our temporal selves and beyond the special properties of visibility. I said to Lynnclaire Dennis, on sending her this poem, that we seem to have a synchronicity across a space of thirty-four years! For I wrote this poem in 1962 when I was sixteen years old and in a state of wonder with pendulums, oscillations, music, and the mysteries of the relationship between mathematics and the physical world. The pendulums traced patterns in the sand (literal and photographic) that are the shadows (in the right choice of frequencies) of her Pattern. Later, I studied knots and, as all knot theorists know, came to understand that knot theory is actually the contemplation of the simplest knotted loop. That loop is the topological form of the orbit of the central sphere in Lynnclaire's Pattern. For me the Pattern is not The Pattern (the Tao that can be told is not the eternal Tao). It is Nothing Special and therefore very precious indeed.

—Louis Kauffman
Department of Mathematics
University of Illinois at Chicago

FOREWORD

by Joan Borysenko, Ph.D.

The remarkable sequence of near-death experiences, dreams, and synchronicities through which Lynnclaire brought back the Pattern from the world of Spirit is a fascinating story. And like all good stories, it makes us think. What is the Pattern and how does it relate to the way in which we live our lives?

The Nechung Medium of Tibet considers the Pattern a *terma*, a hidden treasure, meant to be disclosed to the world at this time. Some physicists believe that it may provide a template for generating clean energy—a kind of perpetual motion machine. Religious leaders are amazed that the symbols of every major religion, and of many indigenous spiritual traditions, are present in the Pattern's many perspectives. Colleagues interested in energy medicine—based on the *chi* or life force that flows through the acupuncture meridians—are intrigued with the possibilities that the Pattern may hold for healing.

While it will be some time before research can uncover the Pattern's potential, the very story of its "discovery" may prove to be its greatest gift. As you read about the ten-year odyssey that accompanied the Pattern's manifestation, and the remarkable connections that it spawned between the unlikeliest people, you will be reminded that miracles do happen, and that the greatest miracle of all is love.

Lynnclaire is like a wise and funny next-door neighbor continually pondering the question, "Why me?" Why was she chosen to bring back the Pattern? Her eventual revelation "Why not me?" is a message to us all. Each one of us is linked to one another and to Spirit. Each one of us has a potential that we may never have dreamed of. And when we are willing to give ourselves to love's service, our very life becomes the source of miracles.

The opening line of *A Tale of Two Cities* reads, "It was the best of times, it was the worst of times." So it is in the late twentieth century. Advances in technology have eradicated smallpox and created test-tube babies. The world is linked in a web of lightning-fast communication that puts knowledge instantly at our fingertips. But what of wisdom? Is it wise to destroy the rain forests, wipe out indigenous cultures, pollute the air and water with toxins that mutate our DNA, and invest billions of dollars in technologies capable of wreaking instantaneous destruction? Why is it that in the United States, one of the wealthiest countries on earth, the incidence of depression is ten times greater than it was fifty years ago?

As many spiritual traditions have observed, whatever we do to the earth or to one another, we do to ourselves. The fact that everything in this universe is interconnected and interdependent is inherent in the wild and spooky world of quantum physics. Albert Einstein once observed that the idea that we are separate from one another is an "optical delusion of consciousness." The greatest challenge of our time is to unite the promise of technology with the life of Spirit—the inherent connectedness between things—so that love and compassion create a milieu out of which a new epoch in human history can arise. I believe that Lynnclaire's remarkable odyssey with the Pattern, a deceptively simple geometrical form consisting of three interlocking loops, contains the hope of just such a new world.

Joan Borysenko is a Harvard-trained research scientist with a Ph.D. in anatomy and cellular biology. She is the president of Mind/Body Health Sciences, Inc., in Boulder, Colorado, and the author of the bestselling books Minding the Body, Mending the Mind *and* Guilt Is the Teacher, Love Is the Lesson.

$\mathcal{P}$ R E F A C E

$\mathcal{N}$ot a single experience in my life prepared me for death, yet it was my death—technically, a near-death experience—that awakened me to my purpose and prepared me to truly live my life.

On New Year's Eve 1986, I was at the Hofburg Palace in Vienna, Austria, living one of my childhood fantasies—I was "Cinderella," dancing with my dashing "prince" at the Kaiser Ball. Never did I imagine that only a fortnight later I would be dancing the dance of life, waltzing between the worlds.

On January 15, 1987, as I was soaring seventeen thousand feet over the Austrian Alps in a hot-air balloon, the Angel of Death descended like a thief in the night, an oxygen-consuming fireball blazing through my body. For me the Angel of Death was an incredible being of Light, gathering me in wings of clear light for initiation into Eternity. Where moments before I had been surrounded by the majestic peaks of the Alps, suddenly I was suspended in an interim of time and space halfway around the world. Now on the summer slopes of Mt. Rainier in the state of Washington, I moved through a field of unity, harmony, and peace. During this interval, I stepped into "the tunnel" and began moving toward the Light. At the end of that darkened passageway, I took one step into the void and left my right footprint embedded in Eternity.

It was there that I saw the "Pattern," the holographic matrix I knew was the single strand of Divine Essence used to weave the tapestry of all creation. It was and is the Light that is the dynamic suchness of Love. It was and is the energetic Truth that seeds the genesis of all beingness. Its design was so complexly simple that I knew it could only have been fashioned in the exalted intricacy of infinity.

Never did I imagine that it would take years to recover my physical, emotional, and spiritual health so that I would be free to remember exactly what I had seen. For four years I talked about the experience and the Pattern, drawing stars, hearts, crosses, eights, threes, pyramids, diamonds, circles, cubes, straight lines, spirals up and spirals down, rectangles, and crescents—every shape you can imagine—insisting they were all the same. I struggled to remember the Pattern, yet its full retrieval took more than seven years.

I am humbled that I am the one to share this Pattern with the world. In these pages you will see that my life has not been much different from yours. My sorrow is your sorrow. My pain mirrors yours and so, too, do my anger, laughter, and fears. Why me? I guess the only answer is that perhaps the universe knew that if I ever remembered it, I would talk about it.

As a universal symbol, containing symbols from diverse spiritual traditions, the Pattern is intensely personal, evoking an amazing spectrum of responses from individuals. As a midwife to the Pattern and the author of this book, I share only *my* story, my inner knowings, and my hope.

But bear in mind that this *is* a true story.

Were these experiences happenstance, or were they providence? Can so many shared episodes be flukes of fate? Are our lives constructed by layer upon layer of coincidence? Are what we term "unusual" events random anomalies on an otherwise predictable screen? Is life merely a span of years composed of a series of chance encounters? Are our encounters with God, angels, or guides supernatural, or are they merely natural? Are the moments of awe that touch our souls miracles, or are they ordinaries? And perhaps the most existential question of all: Does life really present us an opportunity to live and love w-holy and fully with joy?

Perhaps the Pattern offers a clue to many of these queries, if not an answer.

As you read, please keep an open mind and heart, for I believe it *is* possible that within these pages you may encounter a universal piece of self. As poet Judith Morley reminds us in her book *Miss Laughinghouse & The Reluctant Mystic,* "The task is to live in the Mystery and celebrate the unknowing."

—Lynnclaire Dennis

Note: As the Pattern continues to make its way around the world, it is being explored by many, both by individuals interested in personal growth and by those in what are usually perceived to be the discrete disciplines of science and spirit. I look forward to sharing those impressions with you in the near future. I also would love for you to share with me what the Pattern means to you and how it has effected any change in your mind, heart, or life.

To contact me, please write c/o EPI, P.O. Box 152, Tiburon, CA 94920.

To order additional copies of the book and other products associated with the Pattern, kindly refer to the ordering information at the end of the book.

A Call to Oneness

This work is a call to Oneness, not merely the work or story of one person. It is dedicated to those who believe that war has never been a catalyst to lasting peace. It is in honor of those who dare to imagine, dream, and co-create a new world, a world at peace.

Because of these individuals—individuals who choose to make the ascent of personal transformation—I believe that one day the global human family and Gaia will be restored to unity.

For the sake of the world's children, may we each grow to respect and honor our uniqueness, even as we celebrate our Goddessential sameness.

Someday, after mastering the winds, the waves, the tides
  and gravity,
We shall harness for God the energies of love,
And then, for the second time in the history of the world,
Man will discover fire.

—Pierre Teilhard de Chardin

C H A P T E R   O N E

Cosmic Bloopers

Grim Fairy Tales: Tales That Are Far from Fair

*M*y retrieval and remembrance of
the Pattern were directly connected to a lifelong search for happiness, a
quest to find the sense and meaning of my life. This pursuit focused
primarily around finding the *perfect* life partner, the other half who
would make me feel whole. This was a journey I embarked upon at a
very tender age . . .

Surely, some of you remember the tales of Mr. Peabody, the intellectual pooch, and his boy Sherman from the *Rocky and Bullwinkle* cartoons. Their adventures were sort of like a prehistoric *Quantum Leap*.
Sherman was the quintessential prepubescent intellectual, a scrawny
kid whose favorite pastime was traveling with his Houdini Peabody in
his wondrous Wayback Machine. I would watch in amazement as
Sherman and Mr. Peabody zapped backward and forward through time,
mesmerized (to say nothing of jealous) as they magically headed into
the past or zipped off into the future. However, on occasion our heroes

1

would find themselves tarred and feathered, or boiled in oil, the suckers and soon-to-be-sacrificial lambs in some historical snafu. Their trips often included rewriting or re-righting history.

Well, there I sat, spellbound over my soggy Cheerios, holding my breath, even though I knew full well that a fraction of a second before their seemingly inevitable demise they would receive cosmic help and zap back to the present through the Wayback Machine.

All of this is to say that when it came to relationships of the intimate variety, there were days I wished I had a Wayback Machine or thought I should change my name to "Sherman." Like others, I was constantly beseeching the heavenly deities to bring me back from the brink of some romantic or emotional twilight zone.

To understand where we're going—into the unknown—all of us must come to closure on our stories, on the past that has lurked just over our shoulders, keeping our full awareness outside the here and the now. Once we realize that our story is just that, a story, we are free to create anew.

And thus begins my story.

A Cabbage Patch, a Stork, or the Zygote Fairy?

Looking back, I realize that, like the Sherman and Mr. Peabody cartoons, a great many of my childhood memories are mentally tattered as a result of being spun through the proverbial time machine—my brain. But more than a few are entirely intact, especially my childhood suspicions regarding my true parentage. From an early age I believed that on the day I was born I was kidnapped from the hospital nursery. For years I held hope that my *real* family was out there frantically searching for me and would eventually find me. Of course they would live in a distant castle or at least have lifetime passes to Disneyland.

Adopted? No Way. I *knew* this could never be, because a buddy who *was* adopted told me that all her life she felt *special* because she'd been chosen. Never in my wildest imagination would I have used words like *special* and *chosen* to describe my life.

If you were to interview all the children in *any* family, you would likely come away swearing that there was no possible way they were related. Based on these interviews, you might conclude that each kid had different parents, different siblings, and grew up in a different home, if not on a different planet.

Nowhere was this more true than in my own family.

Not long ago I was listening to an audiocassette of the book *Women Who Run with the Wolves*. In it, Dr. Clarissa Pinkola Estés shares a wonderful theory she calls the phenomenon of "The Mistaken Zygote." In her soothing voice she explains what she thinks happened to those of us who've felt all our lives that we did not belong where we were. Finally—a theory that explained to my adult mind what had happened! Suddenly I understood how I had landed in my family.

In this brilliant hypothesis of profound emotional reasoning, Dr. Estés explains how one is brought to Earth for a human incarnation. Forget the stork. The human egg of essence is carried in a basket, flown through the universe to planet Earth on the mystical wings of the Zygote Fairy! It is this semiangelic sprite's job to deliver this precious bundle to the special couple whom the gods have predetermined are this soul's *perfect* parents.

Well, it seems that more than a few of us were so excited about coming to Earth that during the trip we were jumping up and down with joy. Even though we were told repeatedly to keep our seat belts fastened, we just had to see where we were going, and just as the Zygote Fairy was making her last low turn, we were accidentally bounced right out of the basket. To make a sad story short, we fell head over heels to Earth, landing a tad short of our intended destination.

When I heard this, I remember thinking, "No doubt about it. I wasn't adopted, and I'm not an alien. *I'm a mistaken zygote!*"

Loco Motives

It has taken me a long time to figure out that family members' feelings about historical reality are seldom—if ever—the same. I honor the truth that no one is ultimately right or wrong in her or his recollection of familial history. Each of us sees life through our personal filters and we experience it from our own unique perspective. No two people will feel and process the same event in the same way. So, some members of my family may recall the following events differently.

That said, like all members of the human species, I've had core issues—hard core at that—that took root and sprouted within my family of origin. As I said previously, nothing in my life—religious or otherwise—prepared me for the death that changed my life.*

When I was five my father had an exchange with a local preacher that led to his religious conversion, a transmutation from agnostic to apostle. This shift would take him beyond active alcoholism to seminary and, eventually, into the ministry.

Tragically—from my perspective—Daddy was often so heavenly minded that there was little left of him to share with his earthly family. I believe that religion was in many ways his attempt to nullify his sorrow, guilt, and pain, a way to fill the fathomless sucking void he felt within himself. In many ways the only thing that changed in my dad's life was his drug of choice. He became a pusher and was committed to meeting other people's needs while denying his own. It was my sad experience, however, that for the most part, "other people" did not include his family. His new addiction consisted of creating an environment where he was loved and indispensable, a place that was always away from home. The closest times I had with my father were when I got to accompany him on trips.

---

* Interesting aside: In 1994 when Terrence McKenna saw the Pattern, he asked me what drug I'd been using when I saw it. When I told him, "No drugs; it's what I saw when I died," his response was—"Ultimate trip!"

Having learned early on that getting along meant conforming to "the Faith of Our Fathers"—specifically, to "the faith of *my* father"—I became the dutiful daughter, doing what others wanted me to do, clueless as to my authentic self. To obtain his approval, I cultivated submissiveness, the character trait deemed most virtuous in this context.

As it is for many, growing up was for me a survival test. Consequently I have spent most of my life preoccupied with safety. There were times I felt that living in my *nuclear* family was like living through a reactor meltdown. Certainly any glow I radiated was the result of poisonous verbal fallout, *not* the result of overexposure to love.

When my mother looks back at my father's conversion on that fateful night in 1956, she will only say that, "For over eight years I'd gone to bed with my Burt Reynolds, and one morning I discovered I had woken up beside a Billy Graham."

Like my mother, the kids had no choice but to go for the ride. I was still very young when I realized that at some level my family was aboard a LOCO-motive—one whose engineer was definitely loco and whose motives were highly suspect. In one fell swoop, the father I adored had turned the control of our lives over to a heretofore unknown God and a church they called the "Chicken Coop." Dad saw his job as shoveling coal—a.k.a. faith—into the boiler. Sadly, the caboose was where feelings and family resided, and the train ran with or without the caboose. Without a doubt the line our family was initially scheduled to run on had been switched, and I for one was emotionally derailed. It would be years before I would get my life on track again.

Fit to Be Tied in Thou Shalt Knots

As a result of my father's conversion there was a lot of talk in my family about heaven and hell, and believe me, the weight of the emphasis was on the heat of the flames, not the warmth of the Light. More often than not, I was at the altar seeking alteration.

In spite of religious doctrine to the contrary, I soon came to the conclusion that hell had to be right here on Earth. At least I hoped it was, because if this *wasn't* it, then the real hell must be unimaginable.

Over the years, in addition to memorizing the hymnal and huge passages of the Bible, I mastered religious dogmas, the core one being "God (via the Bible) said it. Therefore you *will* believe it, and that settles it." End of discussion. This meant that any point of view different from the tenets of our particular denomination was closed to further investigation. Taboos included science, history, alternative spiritual paths, and experiential evidence that might support any contradictory thought or belief system.

At the tender age of five my greatest joy was dancing. But then came the Saturday morning following my father's metamorphosis when I was told I would not be going to dance class anymore. Apparently this was due to an eleventh commandment Moses had forgotten to write down when he was taking dictation—"Thou shalt not dance."

Our denomination held the belief that dancing was a "sin." It became the first of many "evils" eliminated from my life. Not only had the ribbons of my ballet slippers been cut; at the same time the life-sized dancing doll that was my fifth birthday present also disappeared. My sense of self had been nipped in the bud, and my rising star fell into a sea of despair where it was quickly extinguished.

Put into the foxhole on the front lines of an unholy war where others fought to control my thoughts and curtail my actions—all in the name of breaking my will—I began to accumulate scars I soon saw as defects of my soul. Repeatedly I suffered wounds that were self-inflicted as I sacrificed my life and will on the altar of *perfection*.

Over and over I struggled in vain to win and maintain approval. By the ripe old age of ten I had given up on ever figuring out who I really was and found myself stuck atop a pedestal where I was expected (by myself, of course) to be the "perfect preacher's kid." How come no one ever clued me in on the fact that everyone else *expected* preachers' kids to be the worst of the lot?

From this lofty perch all I could do was contemplate a long fall, so I attempted to maintain my balance. I accepted without argument the role others assigned me, believing that this was the only way I might survive. My life became intricately linked to doing what others wanted or needed me to do, and I was regularly assured that this behavior was synonymous with God's will for my life. I figured that agreement *at any cost* was the only way to circumvent the anger, rejection, and the wholesale abandonment that followed any self-assertion.

My modus operandi became manifest in my personalized acronym for fear—"Forget Everything And Run." I was terrified at what would happen if I ever dared to wade into the psychological muck and emotional mire that kept me stuck—but alive—in my survival patterns. There was no way I wanted to go through what I was convinced would be a prolonged and vexatious "dying" if I ever really contemplated change. Avoiding change was my credo. Heaven knew—I knew—that I would go down in flames if I ever let myself feel my anguish, or God forbid, my anger. I was not afraid of death, but I was terrified that the energy of my emotions might provoke others' anger—specifically my Dad's—and kill *them*. I never saw that it was the suppression of *their* feelings that was slowly killing me. As a result I was scared to death to truly live.

By the time I was eighteen, approval was so critical to my sense of self that I went to Bible college simply to avoid a battle and appease my father. It was here that for the first time in my life I rebelled in a significant way—but only after being told by the president of the college that God had "convicted [sic] him that it was a sin for women to wear pants; therefore, all women students would immediately send all jeans and slacks home." Needless to say, I didn't last long.

Two years later I capitulated to my father's will again, this time going so far as to marry the man he chose for me.

Martyrdom: The Execution of the Soul

Following our marriage, my husband and I went into the ministry, joining the staff of a religious collegiate organization, where for seven years we role-modeled to cursedly near perfection a toxic amalgam of our dysfunctional, fear-based families of origin. Like my mother, I existed in emotional silence and psychological denial, following the law not only to the letter but to the punctuation mark as well. I married my husband as a way of obeying the commandment to "honor thy father." Afterward, I thought I could earn even more spiritual merit by fully complying with my marriage vow. I had actually said that I would "obey" my husband. As I abdicated all self-responsibility I grew to despise and unconditionally disrespect the person I was forced to confront in the mirror every day.

Since I was five all I had wanted to be was *perfect*—the perfect daughter, the faultless friend, a good sister, and a 4.0 student. Then at twenty I took on the role of the perfect wife—and failed. At twenty-one I found myself pregnant and with grave trepidation was forced to take on the assignment of being the perfect mother. I failed again. No matter what I did, I could not get it right. The only logical conclusion was that I was not only a fraud, as I had often thought I was, I was damaged goods, defective in spirit and deficient in worthiness. I figured I must have been standing in the wrong line when God handed out the most basic skill required to live on planet Earth—the ability to meet everyone's needs and expectations.

For a decade I pleaded for help, but the only place I was allowed to look was within the context of the church. When no real help was forthcoming, I amended my daily prayer to "Give me this day my daily delusion."

By 1978 I knew I would never be able to be perfect. I had also figured out that no one really cared. After seven years of marriage all I wanted was to die.

Almost overnight my desire to die was transformed into the *will* to die, and not surprisingly, my body began to cooperate. However, I was—tenacious to the end—determined to die perfectly. That meant that all my secrets, guilt, and shame must remain concealed. I never had to contemplate anything so crass as suicide, since my health was crumbling as fast as my will to live. Long before the medical community began to explore the mind-body health link I was demonstrating it, as my body honored my intention to die an honorable, *natural* death. I calculated, in a detached and rational way, that my death would be spiritually acceptable, bringing no shame on my family. As a matter of fact, dying meant I could be *perfect*. You see, I had it all worked out—I was going be the perfect *martyr*. I knew that those I left behind would inscribe on my grave marker immortal words of virtue that even time would have a hard time erasing. They would carve in stone the words, *Here lies our beloved Lynnclaire. She was the perfect daughter, sister, wife, mother, and friend. May she rest in Eternal Peace.*

If I had anything to say about it, I would go into eternity remembered as perfect—only because it is in poor taste to speak ill of the dead.

However, by grace I aborted this plan on September 17, 1982, when a wise doctor walked into my hospital room, sat down on my bed, and asked, "Lynnclaire, what would you like me to say at your funeral a year from now?"

My first thought was relief, my second gratitude. "Is it cancer?" I hopefully whispered. There would be nothing more sympathy engendering than the unspeakable "C" word. I knew that it would be over soon.

Amazingly, this audacious and compassionate doctor dared to take a giant leap beyond the rigid boundaries of conventional medicine and his own religious beliefs. "No, Lynnclaire," he said, "you don't have cancer. But if you continue on the present course you will soon."

From deep in his heart he summoned the courage to lift the veil of illusion I had pulled around my life and marriage. He dared to suggest that maybe, just maybe, there were other solutions to my pain. I will never forget his saying, "Lynnclaire, you *don't* have to die. You only have to decide what *you* want."

What? Could what I wanted have anything remotely to do with what God wanted? Was it possible that all God wanted from me was to do whatever made me happy?

His words made no sense and implied a concept so thoroughly foreign to my way of thinking that even contemplating it terrified me. I was aghast and knew my family would be scandalized if I heeded the advice—actually the medical order—that followed. Knowing that I was powerless to effect change in any way short of dying, he told me he had asked a psychiatrist to interview me. Furthermore, said shrink would be there within the hour.

Meeting with this doctor, I broke down and openly wept for the first time in years. As tears flowed from my eyes and pain poured from my heart, layer upon layer of agony peeled from my soul.

Immediately the flimsy fabric of my marriage began to unravel, and almost overnight my ten-and-a-half-year marriage disintegrated. With it succumbed the illusions of white picket fences and happily-ever-afters.

I found myself spiritually and emotionally excommunicated, abandoned by the only support system I had ever known. This rejection and abandonment shook me to my core. However, it also caused an eruption within me from which fountained a raging will to live. My motivations may not have been altogether righteous, but they surely kept me alive.

Tragically, when the illusion I had built up around my sham-filled and shameful marriage shattered, my entire family was cut by flying shards of blame, and we have all bled for a long, long time. In the years following the divorce, there were many times I wondered if it might not have been easier for everyone—especially the children—if I had died. For sadly, as in any divorce, the losers in this chain reaction of emotional deceit and denial were the children. It remains my heart's desire that one day love will lead to forgiveness, and compassion will free us to befriend one another's spirit.

CHAPTER TWO

Parting the Veil

We know that all religious aspiration, all sincere worship, can have but one source and goal. We know that the God of the educated and the God of the child, the God of the civilized and the God of the primitive, is after all the same God; and that this God does not measure our difference, but embraces all who live rightly and humbly on earth.

—Ohiyesa (Charles Alexander Eastman)
The Soul of an Indian

Separating the Magic from Illusion

I realize only in retrospect that from birth my foot was placed on an unusual path. My earliest dreams often left me with intuitive knowings that were frightening. Repeatedly, throughout my youth, I found myself on inner sojourns that revealed startling intuitions borne out in the next day's experience.

However, rather than being acknowledged as real, my premonitions and perceptions were crushed by the vehement denial and the fervid prayers of my father. Over time I learned to keep quiet and shoved these episodes into the darkest recesses of my comatose consciousness.

11

I knew that punishment for doing otherwise would be swift. If I did not maintain my inherited Scandinavian stoic silence, my emotional rejection and spiritual abandonment would be nothing less than complete.

Little did I dream that this psychic gift my father so eschewed in me was one that had caused him staggering pain. There was no way I could know, let alone understand, that his reactions came from a heart overflowing with the loving intent of protection. Never did I imagine that these psychic experiences would be a form of preparation for the day I would make a spiritual leap, hurdling even my father's faith and all the exclusionary religious tenets that I had so long espoused.

The most dramatic of these psychic experiences occurred on June 25, 1977, when my father suffered a massive heart attack while free diving at Makena Landing on the island of Maui. He died before reaching the surface.

At that exact moment, I was driving down Mt. Rainier with my husband and daughter, following an overnight visit to Paradise Lodge, the century-old inn nestled high in the alpine meadows. Since we had just estimated the travel time to Spokane, our intended destination, the exact timing of the following events has always been certain.

Without warning, I was overcome with chest pain and was unable to breathe. Somehow I knew I was dying. I demanded that my husband stop the car and let me out, and when he balked, refusing to pull over because of the narrow shoulder and hairpin turns, I threatened to open the door and jump. Only then did he take me seriously and stop the car. He was dumbfounded, watching helplessly as I slid down the side of the mountain, falling through the loose gravel even as I fought for every breath. Breathless between gasps, I earnestly prayed the pain would stop or that God would let me die quickly.

I have never doubted that I psychically shared my father's death experience. I believe that somehow, due to the depth of a multi-incarnational connection, I was viscerally, if not cognitively, with him during his transition. Yet, an indecipherable sense of foreboding kept me from knowing the truth. I believe a kind of psychic cocoon engulfed me, protecting me from seeing him or otherwise knowing what was happening to him.

When the pain ceased I returned to the car, overwhelmed by the need to go home immediately. I asked my husband if we could abandon our plans to make an overnight stop. This thought ruled my mind with the tyranny of the urgent. However, he was equally adamant that we keep a commitment and arrive home unannounced the following morning as part of a long-planned surprise. Although I remained steadfast in my insistence that we go straight to the home of my friends, my husband, of course, prevailed.

Later that afternoon we checked into our hotel, and within the hour the local police tracked us down, and my friends arrived to break the news of my father's death.

I find it somehow ludicrous that in spite of these occasional, powerful experiences, I continued to voluntarily commit intellectual suicide. My self-esteem was so superficial that I allowed those who possessed advanced degrees, proclaiming themselves to be of ecclesiastical superiority, to perform somatic liposuction on my soul. Again, it was only decades later that I realized I had relinquished my ability to reason as regularly as I put both my heart and my dollars into the offering plate. I had no idea how to break the stultifying emotional silence and shatter my old "commandments."

It would take a lesson called "death" before I learned that I possessed the strength to sever the chains of obligation that had so long bound my mind, suffocated my spirit, and throttled my voice.

Climbing the Corporate Ladder: Hung by Rung

When I dared to cross an emotional, psychic, or mental bridge, I did so because I was coerced. Only when threatened by a catastrophic

flood of tears, abandonment, or someone else's rage could I be compelled to move to the other side of an issue.

Never was this more true than in 1982 and the years that followed
my divorce.

It was an incredible shock to find myself single and unemployed.
Having been a missionary for seven years, for all intents and purposes I
had no career or employment history. However, I quickly decided that
living below the poverty level for thirty years was enough and that the
perfect solution was to become the consummate (read perfect) busi-
nesswoman. I resolved to do whatever it would take to achieve financial
success so that I could be independent. I vowed that I would never again
have to depend on another person for anything, or ever have to ask
permission.

Following the unlocking of my wedlock, I immediately went out
and bought the best "running suit" I could afford and headed for the
fast track. Hunger, fear, and the need to pay for a roof over my head
were powerful motivators.

Miraculously, within a week I was gainfully employed and quickly
established a niche in the sales and marketing arena of the burgeoning
telecommunications industry. Once I knew my way around the course,
I moved to the inside passing lane, where I set a track record for veloc-
ity—running in high heels, no less.

Before long the financial scoreboard clearly showed I was winning.
In less than two years, I was proud owner of an array of impressive
trophies and material toys. However, the fleeting pleasure I got from
these possessions evaporated into loneliness.

I then reasoned that the only way to alleviate the ache where I
thought my soul was supposed to be was to accumulate the newer, bigger, and supposedly better model. I continued a relentless campaign to
amass more things, hoping that they would fill the void I had heretofore filled through religion. Soon I was a custodian to stuff and a full-
time administrator to my continuing inner crisis. I was divorced, out of

the situation that kept me in a box, yet I was still stuck on the merry-go-round of perfection. I was out in the open, spinning round and round, and still going nowhere. Fast.

All this was done in search of the elusive something or someone that would make me a happy, perfect person.

Fishing for solutions in what I considered to be the vast ocean of mind, I kept snagging my hook on the bottom. More than once I pulled up a waterlogged boot of "wouldas, shouldas, and couldas," shoes that still had a swift kick or two left in them. Although I was clueless about what it was I wanted, I kept getting caught up in expectations attached to a specific result. I was paralyzed by irrational fears, especially the fear that what I thought I wanted was the wrong thing.

I guess my greatest fear was that everything inside of me was psychic quicksand, that my squirrel-caged thoughts were leading me deeper into psychological muck and spiritual mire.

Eventually, I realized there was no heart or soul satisfaction in owning a new top-of-the-line Mercedes or two beautiful condominiums. Designer clothes only served as armor to keep my insecurity from showing through, and flying in private jets, cruising on luxury yachts, or drinking Dom Perignon through a straw just perpetuated an illusory myth that material things could fill what I reluctantly conceded was a spiritual vacuum.

Yet, at that point in my life, I saw nowhere else to go, even though I knew that I was going to arrive at the same destination—nowhere—sooner, if I stayed on the fast track. The only advantage I had on this course was that I knew the rules of survival.

As a thirty-four-year-old "child" I knew that I might not have had the happiest childhood but that it certainly had been a long one. My earliest fantasies had survived into adulthood, and countless times I found myself still asking, "Who am I? Who are these people? How on earth did I get here?" In my darkest moments of silent doubt, I wondered if there really was a God. If there was, I was sure that my tenure on planet Earth as a human being must be his or her idea of a practical joke. I was terrified that one day I was going to wake up, walk around a corner, and some cosmic joker would jump out and scare the daylights out of me, shouting, "Boo! Smile! You're on Karmic Camera!"

Riding the Winds of Change

At the deepest level of my being I felt like half a person, and consequently I felt destined to spend my entire life looking for my other half if I were ever to fulfill my longing to feel whole.

By the summer of 1986, in spite of one colossal faux pas in matrimony and several minor catastrophes in romance, I remained among the last of the hopeful romantics, still believing that relationship could be "elationship." Time and again, I seemed to find myself on a flight through one emotional twilight zone or another, hollering for some cosmic Mr. Peabody to rescue me and magically bring me home.

That summer an acquaintance set me up on a blind date while I was on a business trip to Chicago. Instantly, something in the male-female dance that my date, Steve, and I found ourselves doing was different. For the first time, I was taking a rational, nonemotional approach to relationship. We had both been through painful marriages and agonizing divorces and had had more than our share of distressing and depressing experiences in romance. This new style of behavior based in logic and experience seemed, without a doubt, a safer course to take. Almost immediately we joined hands and jumped into a committed relationship. It would be a long while before either of us realized we were in way over our heads.

I honor both of us, however, and believe that on a deep intuitive level we knew we were together for some not-yet-revealed higher purpose.

Unfortunately, getting to this purpose would require my "death," and the cosmic/karmic plan would not be long in revealing itself.

The first disaster came a month before our wedding, the day the engraved invitations went in the mail. It was the perfect day for my fiancé's as-good-as-but-not-quite-ex-wife to refuse to sign their final divorce papers. Deposits were forfeited, my gown went into storage— never to be seen again—and what would have been the quintessential wedding of the eighties was rescheduled for the next Valentine's Day.

In many ways, it was as if from the onset of our relationship some Cosmic Grand Marshall had thrown out a first ball and proclaimed, "Let the games begin!"

We were both blind to the well-established patterns we had designed in order to survive within the context of intimate relationships. I was again engaged in a situation in which I would have to struggle to win approval by playing one mental, spiritual, or emotional game after another. These were games where the competition was fierce and often ruthless, and there was little in the way of cooperation.

Sadly, when I sensed I was losing, forfeiting myself, I discovered it was not that I didn't know how to play—it was simply that there were no rules and we had to make them up as we went along.

This time the fight would be to the finish, for once again in my heart and mind I had already made the vow, promising "until death do us part."

Little did I know the death would be mine and that it would come so soon.

The Kaiser Ball and a Dancing Doll

I've often wondered where the word *honeymoon* came from. I have decided that it was named thus because for so many relationships, including both of mine, it is a sticky situation in the dark!

In spite of having to call off our wedding, Steve and I left for our scheduled month-long honeymoon in Europe. Magic was planned for this trip, the highlights being the Kaiser Ball at the Hofburg Palace on

New Year's Eve and the International High-Altitude Balloon Race across the Alps.

As darkness fell on New Year's Eve, I descended the elegant staircase of Vienna's famous Imperial Hotel like Cinderella, sweeping into the elegant lobby dressed in the most exquisite creation I had ever owned. Outside, we stood beneath a canopy of stars, enveloped in a cloud of romantic fantasy before we were whisked away to the palace to celebrate the dawning of a new life.

Entering this elegant castle, I was immediately aware that the walls were drenched in history. I could feel the spirits of Emperor Franz Joseph and Empress Maria Theresa floating among the throng. Walking alone down the long hallways, I listened as the stones and walls whispered secrets to my heart. I heard the ancient echo of children's laughter, and with every step I felt seen and met by spirits of the past. That night my essence and experience were engraved in those walls, to be forever held in place by the mortar of my dreams. With each turn of every dance, I earnestly hoped that nostalgia alone would be enough to keep this enchantment alive.

My life was soon to take another turn, one far more dizzying than any I danced that night. Within days the illusions that had comprised the new foundation of my life began to crumble—including the magic concocted that night.

On New Year's Day, the coldest winter in one hundred years began to rampage across the continent, forcing us to sit still for more than a week. When the sun rose on January 10, we were more than ready for the next step on our itinerary—to rendezvous with the Goddess of the Wind and soar on her wings.

Concurrent Realities: The Breath of Dragons

Every January, balloon enthusiasts from all over the world converge on a selected Austrian hamlet for the International High-Altitude Balloon Race, a daring race across the Austrian Alps. This was my fiancé Steve's third year to participate in the race.

It is a contest of keen competition, where endurance is combined with audacity and daring. Pilots come to prove their skills and test the competence of their opponents. Together they soar through unpredictable winter skies, only a gust away from disaster at any moment. In their attempt to best Mother Nature, their ambition is to win, their challenge to survive.

Over the course of a week, the objective of these modern-day Montgolfiers is to accumulate the most air miles in the least amount of time while remaining over Austrian soil. The pilots usually fly solo, tethered to the earth only by their two-way radios. A chase crew follows on the ground, their life-or-death task to keep the balloon in constant sight and on course and to pick their pilot up in time for dinner.

Traveling from west to east, pilots attempt to harness, master, and ride the winds, constantly working with their ground crews to stay in Austrian air space. At that time, if a pilot inadvertently crossed into any of the eastern bloc nations, it meant immediate disqualification from the race. In the worst case, such a mistake could also mean imprisonment or death. Remember that prior to 1989 these countries had invisible borders that were aggressively patrolled by gun-toting guards constantly on the lookout for spies or escapees in small planes or balloons.

For four days the weather raged. One pilot, fearing that the storms were ill omens, withdrew his team from the competition. The other pilots, crews, media, and spectators who had gathered from all over the world protested in unison, blustering almost as loudly as the wind. As temperatures dropped to forty degrees below zero, with the wind chill factor multiplying the depth of our discomfort, all we could do was batten down the hatches and turn up our electric blankets.

On the morning of January 14, a desperate couple braved the weather, traveling from Vienna to see Steve, who is a physician, for a professional consultation regarding their nine-year-old son. Several months before, he had found a hidden stash of candy and had his fill. In fact, he had innocently and tragically ingested a huge overdose of illegal drugs his parents had concealed in the sugary concoction. As a result, he suffered serious brain damage that, among other things, left him blind.

It was agonizing to witness as Steve explained to these guilt-ridden, distraught parents that their physicians were telling them the truth: the damage was irreversible, the blindness permanent. He elucidated again exactly how the massive dose of drugs in their son's tiny system had induced an extreme condition known as *catastrophic hypoxia*. During this acute medical crisis, sections of the child's brain had literally starved to death. Lack of oxygen caused him to lapse into a deep coma, in which his heart and breathing had stopped. The brain damage and blindness were caused by the massive and irreversible death of brain cells. Their son's condition was as unalterable as their parental culpability and anguish.

I was in tears as we watched their train pull out, knowing that it was taking the parents and this child of their heart to a destination they had not planned on visiting in this lifetime. Steve and I stood on that platform united in our gratitude for having healthy children and being healthy ourselves.

Jaga Tea or Me?

We returned to the race center, arriving in time for the afternoon pilot's briefing. We entered only to hear Heinz, the event meteorologist, regretfully announce that the updated weather report called for yet another cold front. As darkness fell, all hope of flying once again evaporated.

International flight regulations prohibit pilots, passengers, and their crews from drinking alcoholic beverages within twenty-four hours before flying, and for this reason all participants had resisted the urge to party. Even with the odds for flying as bad as they were, no one wanted to gamble and wind up grounded due to an elevated blood-alcohol level. Until this moment everyone had continued to hope, believing that by some miracle the rising sun would bring about a change of heart in the weather gods.

It appeared there was no such divine reprieve in sight.

Sensing an auspicious moment, one of the major sponsors of the event announced that they would host a party. All the stops were pulled out as they toasted the pilots, flight crews, press, and the assortment of visiting dignitaries. It was a successful effort to cool many of the rising tempers.

For years I had been a teetotaler, but that night I requested a glass of red wine merely to be sociable. The bartender and my friends encouraged me to try a European beverage called jaga tea, assuring me that this brew was a delicious, hot, spiced red wine. It did not take any coaxing to get me to trade a wine glass for a steaming hot mug.

It must have been delicious. I say "must have been" because I do not have more than the vaguest recollection of the evening. Only later did we learn that jaga tea is a European winter version of a potent drink known as Long Island iced tea. The only difference is that the base for jaga tea is a strong red wine instead of iced tea. Like its American cousin, it is liberally laced with many varieties of clear, hard liquor.

The following morning Steve was up early as usual, heading for the daily pilots' briefing that was held snow or shine. At eight o'clock he burst back into our lilliputian room, manic with excitement.

"Lynnclaire! Hurry and get up! You've got to get dressed. We're going to fly," he exclaimed.

"Go away, Steve. Leave me alone," I cried as he rudely pulled the duvet off me. I was desperately ill, and if intentions could kill he would have disintegrated on the spot.

I leaned to the side of the bed and pulled back the draperies. I struggled to focus my eyes, thinking that the frost on the windowpane was so thick that I couldn't see outside.

Wrong. What I could not see through was the blowing snow. Heinz's crystal ball was flawless and he was hitting 100 percent. The blizzard had arrived and we were trapped in a whiteout.

Steve disappeared, but when I heard the shower turn on, I knew I was in trouble.

As he again approached me I resisted. "No. Do not even think about it, Steve. I'm not going anywhere, let alone up in any balloon."

My excitement about the race vanished as the bile rose in my throat. Neither Steve nor I will ever forget the final words that issued from my mouth—"Not in this lifetime."

White Light, or Men in White Jackets?

My momentary reprieve was not long lived. Steve returned, hauled me from the warm feather bed, towed me into the bathroom, and pushed me into a steaming shower.

I was so hung over I could barely stand up. My last supper was not wanting to stay put.

This was not a pretty picture, nor was I what one would call a happy camper. However, I was far too sick to fight.

Steve valiantly tried to assure me, "It's going to be great! There's a tempest on the ground, but Heinz says the ceiling of the storm is only five thousand feet."

Suddenly, I felt remarkably sober, and my brain began to lead a full-scale mutiny.

"Hold on just one minute. I may be impetuous, and I might even still be drunk, but hear me now, and hear me loud and clear. I may be blonde, but Steve, you of all people know I'm not dumb. Do you really think for one blessed minute that I'm going up five thousand feet in this weather in some wicker crate that doesn't even have a lid? That's almost a mile up! Are you nuts?"

Steve continued to laugh as he laced on my snow boots. "Lynnclaire, that's what they mean when they say 'high altitude.' Remember? 'High-Altitude Balloon Race?' Relax, honey. Heinz says that once we break through the clouds we'll be in clear blue sky."

"Someone's high all right, but I think the word you are looking for is *attitude,* not *altitude.* Where's Heinz? I think his brain took a direct lightning hit last night," I snapped.

I knew beyond a shadow of a doubt that I was in big trouble. I knew that if only one balloon went up that day, Steve would be in it, and there was no way in the world he was going to leave me on the ground. Too ill to argue any further, I resigned my protest and retreated into my nausea and silence.

"Lynnclaire, I promise this flight will be one of the highlights of your life, " he vowed.

As my resolve abandoned me, all I could do was surrender. I simply had no energy left for arguing. My mental and physical get-up-and-go had gotten up and gone, so all I could do was reluctantly allow my body to be taken for the ride.

Wandering through the blizzard, we finally located our crew, who were frantically getting everything ready. They were in the final stages of preparation and informed us we would be lifting off in the first wave. Reluctantly, I allowed myself to be hoisted into the basket by Hans, our pilot. As I looked up at the huge golden sphere being inflated over my head, my nausea rose in direct proportion to the height of the flames. The ropes tethering us to the ground were stretched as taut as my nerves.

In this four-by-two-and-a-half-foot basket I was assigned to one corner where virtually no movement was possible due to Steve's ponderous camera equipment and propane and oxygen tanks.

From a nearby balloon, one of the French crew called out to me, "*Au revoir!* Enjoy Heaven, *ma chère.* I will see you for champagne and your hair-burning ceremony when you come back to earth."

This was not the reality check I was looking for. He was referring to what every balloon enthusiast considers a sacred initiation rite—the burning of a hunk of one's hair following one's first flight. Even though this was not my first flight, our friends wanted to make sure it was one I would never forget.

"No thank you very much," I thought sarcastically, muttering to myself, "especially if you think the burning locks are going to be mine."

Biting my tongue, I smiled and waved. These people were mad.

Our ground crew kept us earthbound until we were given clearance to lift off. The clearance came and they released our lifelines. As we began to float, chills went up my spine. "How are we going to penetrate the solid-looking clouds?" I silently wondered. My fear was tinged with curiosity, and I braced myself as we began to slice through the vapors. As we lifted into the haze my queasiness was temporarily pushed aside, supplanted by awe. As the earth fell away, cumulus clouds wrapped us in their opaque, chalky whiteness.

As an eerie hush closed in around us, only the hiss of a phantasmagorical dragon—the propane burner—broke the silence.

The Pendulum Comes to Rest

Abruptly, we perforated the clouds and broke into the heavens, where the morning sky looked as if it had been brushed with the purest blue pigments from the Goddess's paint box. Wondrously, we were encircled by hundreds of mountain peaks, each more spectacular than the last.

It looked as if we were in the center of a penny gumball machine gone berserk, as below us and all around us dozens of brilliantly colored balloons popped through the clouds. Vapors that seconds before appeared as solid as stone now seemed as diaphanous as huge puffs of cotton candy.

For more than an hour we searched for the winds that would nudge us eastward. Although the frigid chill of winter lashed my face, nothing could diminish my growing sense of wonder.

However, I recall the precise moment my left brain sobered up, hollering loudly to get my attention. Someone inside my head was shouting, informing me in no uncertain terms that I had flipped and gone over the edge. Somewhere in that opaque cloud bank it appeared that I had passed through a one-way turnstile of sanity. Why else was I now two miles off the ground (more than ten thousand feet), standing in nothing more than an oversized, squeaky wicker picnic basket? All I knew to do was add an addendum to my rendition of the Lord's prayer, *Give me this day my daily delusion . . . Pleeeeeeasssse, God, I'm too young to die!*

CHAPTER THREE

Like a Thief in the Night

Beyond the Flight of Eagles

*S*everal hours into our flight Steve began to notice that a few things were amiss. His suspicions were deeply rooted in his experience as an air force flight surgeon. First, the communication with our chase crew—which had been intermittent at best—was now nothing but loud bursts of static. However, it was only when Steve realized he was experiencing subtle, but serious, mental difficulties, that he voiced his concerns to Hans, our pilot. He suspected that we were flying *much* higher than we should be without the use of oxygen. Yet when he expressed this concern, Hans replied, "There's no problem. We're only at twelve thousand feet. I fly at this altitude without oxygen all the time."

Unfortunately, Steve and I did not.

Steve again attempted to check in with our chase vehicle and heard nothing but static. Once more Hans assured him that there was no problem, asserting that when we crossed the next ridge everything would be fine.

Seeing that Steve was still not convinced, Hans engaged him in a competition to demonstrate that they were both fine. Steve recounts their conversation as going something like this:

"A sure way to prove you're okay is to do a simple arithmetic problem. So, what's 256 multiplied by 489?"

So much for simple. The verdict as to whether or not there was a problem was definitely in, as they fumbled for the right answer.

During these critical moments the balloon continued to ascend, and in looking back on the situation we later realized that both Steve and Hans were suffering from seriously impaired judgment due to insufficient oxygen to their brains. Soon the balloon had climbed to more than seventeen thousand feet.

No one realized that the hellish nightmare we had witnessed with the young family from Vienna had to some degree become *our* reality. For about fifteen or twenty minutes a greedy vampire had been sucking away not only brain cells, but my life. Death had been stalking me and was now an oxygen-consuming fireball blazing through my body and soul.

Paradise Revisited

I had long since left the balloon and the physical world. I remember hearing Hans say "twelve thousand feet," and it was at that point that my soul took flight, leaving for what was in that instant an unknown destination.

As my life ebbed away, Steve and Hans's voices receded. Looking down on the balloon and my body, I was no longer irritated by the sound of the burner. Nothing of Earth, including the frigid temperature, intruded on the calm and peaceful space I had entered. Relief flooded my mind as my spirit prepared to leave the world behind.

I recall precisely the moment that I broke the bonds of this inimical world and was immersed in the warmth of the Light. Suddenly I was safe, warm, and basking in the luminous sunlight high in the alpine meadows of Mt. Rainier. I was no longer over the Alps—I was in Washington State. Somehow this made perfect sense.

Here, in a place filled with vivid and joyous childhood memories, I took extraordinary comfort in the firmness of the ground beneath my feet. With gratitude and wonder, I wandered through the valley, suffused with a certain knowing that I had crossed a cosmic frontier. Was this Heaven, or was it perhaps some place beyond that celestial otherworld I'd always hoped to be good enough to enter? All I knew—and knew for certain—was that time and space were nothing more than attenuated wisps of human invention. Both were webs of light created by my consciousness.

As my being expanded I saw the cords of years that bound me to the planet. The bond, which was braided from strands of days, bands of months, and ribbons of years, fashioned a nexus between then and now. No doubt this was the mountain of my childhood, but it was essentially different. It was real, yet it was out of sync with the abstraction of linear time. As I stood there I realized that if time was all here now, then it could not be a straight line. This could only mean that there could be no such thing as a beginning, a middle, or an end. Furthermore, it was here that I determined that *I* was out of time as well, even though I had a corporeal existence.

Never before had I considered that there might be such things as coexistent realities. Never had I imagined that there might be concurrent dimensions. Never in my wildest dreams had I thought there might be a way to remember and feel different times and events as if they were happening right now. I realized that in life, death is merely the other side of a threshold over which I could not "normally" see. So, too, in death, life and the land of the "living" were on the other side of a very thin veil.

It struck me that perhaps neither Heaven *nor* Earth is as black or white as I had heretofore believed.

It was then that I looked down at my body and with amazement wondered, "Where did this gown come from?" I was no longer bound in heavy, restricting layers of winter wool, but was wearing an exquisite white gown that appeared to be fashioned of a fabric some master designer had created by splashing star dust on filigree spiderwebs. I watched as it seemed to float above my skin. It was as if a million tiny wings kept it from putting even the weight of a feather on my body. A sense of lightness permeated my being to what I thought must be a cellular—indeed a soulular—level.

And then I heard the MUSIC. It was a tone so sublimely perfect that remembering it still brings me to tears. I knew then, and know now, that I was hearing the symphony of angels, the song of the universe, what some have called the Music of the Spheres. All thoughts melted in its melody and everything else ceased to be of any importance. I closed my eyes and began to dance, moving to the resonant vibration that coursed through my essence. The melody seemed to issue from a single point and was composed of one verse, a song whose mystical tone my entire being knew and sang. I bathed in its melody as utter joy filled my being, and as the sound washed over my spirit, I felt all confusion purged from my consciousness.

Standing beneath this euphonious canopy of grace, I knew love was being awakened at the depths of my soul. Moving with this aria of elegant mercy, I began my return to the dawn of totality as a growing sense of Oneness swelled within my heart, mind, and soul.

The Psalms of My Grandmother

Unspeakable joy filled my heart when I saw my paternal grandmother walking down the mountain. She approached me and enveloped me with open arms. The last time I had seen her was the summer of 1963.

I was eleven when I contracted spinal meningitis, and it was she

who held me as I danced with death for the first time. While I was burning with fever she held me, bathing my face and body with icy cloths as
my frantic parents raced to the hospital. I remember her assuring me
through her tears, "You're going to be fine. Please don't leave us, honey."
My parents always thought it strange that I remembered so much of
this event, because I was unconscious for several days and was one of
the rare survivors of this vicious scourge.

She died shortly thereafter, and due to a regional flood, we were
unable to attend her funeral. As children often do, I felt responsible for
her death. I thought somehow that it was my fault, that her death was
in some way the result of my sickness. No one had ever told me she had
cancer and diabetes. Thus, for decades I carried a burden of guilt. I also
suffered from deep sadness for never getting to say I was sorry. But
most of all, I regretted that I never got to tell her that I remembered
how much she loved me, and how much I loved her.

For more than twenty years I carried an inconsolable grief in my
heart because I never got to say good-bye.

Now we were together again in a magical place where time held no
meaning. As we talked of love, I realized that it alone was real. We walked
hand in hand in a vacuum beyond the boundary we call time. My grief
disappeared as our love was redeemed from what I had believed to be
oblivion. We walked in a sacred space where earthly memory pictures
were hung without physical frames. We traversed a realm that for many
in the here and the now defies logical explanation or reason. Yet, I know
that it is a realm that is exceedingly real. It is a space where grace knows
no bounds and only infinite love abounds. We only have to remember
to make it "real."

In luxuriant warmth we moved on, drawn higher into the valley,
moving toward the Source of the Light. I made a single turn, and the
meadow suddenly became an amphitheater. On a stage that seemed to
be suspended in front of me, I witnessed, with my grandmother, what
seemed to be an encore performance of my life.

Ninety degrees to my right was what I perceived to be a doorway, just within the range of my peripheral vision. It was from this doorway that every character who had played in my life's drama emerged. In turn they walked to center stage, where they faced me. As they greeted me, I inexplicably seemed to understand the highest purpose of our earthly connection. It was love. I saw each person for who he or she was apart from the descriptions I had previously used to define each of them. As they taught me of love, I realized what an important role we play in the development of one another's personality. I saw how judgment, blame, and shame distort or destroy one's sense of self. For the first time I saw the depth of the impression we make on one another's lives.

I was greeted by acquaintances, friends, my grandparents, my father's best friend, as well as a school chum from seventh grade.

One of the most wondrous encounters came when my maternal grandmother approached me carrying a baby. I knew this child was the son I had miscarried in the seventh month of a difficult pregnancy in 1977. Seeing him brought a new peace to my soul as I finally realized that this child of my heart had fulfilled his purpose to absolute perfection. Both then and now, in what was truly a magical moment, his tiny presence awakened a new measure of life within my being. It was only upon this sacred mountain that finally my highest self was endowed with the peace required to end my grief and grant this innocent infant his wings.

A "presence" and Retrospectives of the Past

I soon realized that time is not linear, but rather composed of life's lessons, all of which I had passed through. This panorama flowed over me like a river of living water. As my previously shallow awareness of love and life deepened, I knew that nothing in my life or my death was an accident.

After each person shared his or her message, the meaning of love, each one turned and exited through another door located to the left of the stage. I knew without a doubt that I would soon walk through that door and join them on the other side.

The last person to walk on the stage of my life was a man unknown to me. As he walked to the center of the stage and turned to face me, I noticed that my vision was no longer clear. Although I was certain this was not someone I knew, I could *feel* him at the depths of my soul. He began to speak, communicating directly to my heart. The message he shared that day was engraved on both my mind and my soul: *Lynnclaire, you will be a catalyst for change, for love. You will bring forth, hold, and honor remembrance. You will bring to conscious awareness the realms, realities, and remnants in order that the spirit may remember the dance.*

I knew this was Truth. I also knew that I had never felt so remembered, recognized, understood, or loved. Yet, when he turned to leave, instead of following the others and walking off the stage through the door to my left, he turned toward the right. As I watched him return through the doorway from which he had entered, I clearly recall thinking this was important.

Since that day I've identified him as the *presence.* Suddenly, the stage was gone and I was once again out of time. I was a witness, observing myself as a child. I—she—was dressed in my favorite outfit, blue plaid overalls held up by a pair of bright green elastic suspenders. Around her neck was my most valuable possession, my skate key. I watched as she ran full tilt down the hill, and was surprised to see her stop and pick up a life-sized doll. This was the first time in thirty years that I remembered the gift my parents had given me for my fifth birthday. I watched as my innocent child-self strapped the doll's hands to her hands, and the doll's feet to her feet, and began to dance across the meadows.

Then, as I contemplated this celebration of life, I saw that in a single turn in my-her waltz, I-she was no longer a child, but a thirty-five-year-old woman dancing alone in the Hofburg Palace. Gone were the overalls and suspenders, gone was the doll. I was once more in my magi-cal gown, moving alone in harmony with the MUSIC. In that moment I chose to merge with that self and began to dance. Each step drew me closer to the Light.

Then, in a sacred place somewhere before the Light, I found my-self being held, gently rocked, nurtured, and embraced in the arms of the one I believed to be the *presence*. Whether this was a guide, a guard-ian, a human man who has the ability to walk between the worlds, or even an angel, it does not matter. For still today this memory is alive. The *presence* vibrates within my senses and daily infuses my sentient memory archives with love. I knew then, and remember now, the warmth, serenity, security, and comfort I felt as I was embraced in the arms of a long and still-remembered love. As I was cradled in this se-rene embrace, I was bathed in Light. My spirit was imbued with a sense of peace, and my soul was engraved with the remembrance of a time-less love.

As the experience dissolved into the Light, I found myself again moving higher up the mountain. When I paused to look back into the valley I saw myself as a child again, this time picking a bouquet of wild alpine blooms. As I-she waltzed through the meadow, I heard myself-her singing, calling out to the mountain, "I love you. I love you. I'm home."

I closed my eyes and wondered, "Am I home? Or am I going home?"

A Distant Sea

With my eyes closed, as if in a vision within a vision, I saw my mother. I could not understand why she was there. As far as I knew, my mom was very much alive. Wasn't this "the other side"? I knew I was no longer alive and felt that I was in a space between the worlds.

Yet, as I watched my other, childlike self turn, I heard her ask, "Why can't I see my ocean from here, Mommy?"

Mom's answer was clear. "Oh, Sissy, don't be silly. You can't see the ocean from here. It's too far away."

"Yes, I can," I-she insisted. "I know the ocean's there. It's just behind the clouds. It's my ocean, Mommy. Mine. It *is* there. I *remember*."

When I opened my eyes I was quite surprised that the sea was not in front of me; however, to my amazement, I was now standing face-to-face with my father. There in that sacred space with both him and my grandmother, our communication was nothing less than Holy Communion. Using a language without words, we spoke of the magic. We talked about the mountain beneath our feet and the sea that was just beyond our view.

I will never forget when my dad turned to me and said, "You can see me today." Instantly I knew what he was talking about and recalled again that long trip down the mountain ten years before.

The Cusp of Eternity

It was then that I saw the tunnel and knew with absolute assurance that I was on my way home, certain that the home I had long yearned for was in the Light at the other end of this passageway.

As I was standing alone with my grandmother, she told me that I must make this part of the journey alone. Filled with peace, I knew I would see her again on the other side.

I was ready, and without hesitation took my first step into the corridor that led toward the Light, crossing an intersection that connected now with forever.

A Race against Perpetuity

While I was completing my transitional dance with the illusion of death, in another reality halfway around the world, Steve continued to argue with Hans about our need for oxygen. Finally, Hans capitulated and they began trying to identify which of the tanks contained oxygen. It was only then that they made an appalling discovery. In the chaotic rush to take advantage of the tiny open window in the weather front that morning, the oxygen tanks that were required to be on board had been left on the ground.

By this time several hours had passed since our chase crew had lost contact with us. We were a pending disaster, as no one had been able to alert Hans to the fact that we were drifting dangerously on a northeasterly course. If this heading went uncorrected, the prevailing winds would carry us toward the Czechoslovakian border. We were later told the others were afraid that even if we went down on Austrian soil a rescue attempt would be impossible, as the weather was deteriorating, with another storm rapidly closing in.

Even after discovering there was no oxygen on board, Hans did not descend. Steve continued to grow more concerned about oxygen deprivation and finally decided to interrupt my supposed reverie and make sure I was not having any trouble.

Both he and Hans were oblivious to my condition, as when I lost consciousness my head had fallen against the suede-covered support bar in the corner and remained upright. Because the auxiliary propane tanks and massive film gear wedged my body into a permanent half-seated position, I couldn't fall or even slump over.

When I did not respond to his barrage of questions, Steve grabbed me, turned me around, and with horror found I had no vital signs. Helpless, he and Hans witnessed the final shudder—the seizure of death—as the last of my life left my body.

The tenuous thread of life had broken and I was released.

Steve knew there was no possible way to get my head below my heart because of all the equipment, and with dismay he realized that at this altitude cardiopulmonary resuscitation was futile. Giving up his fight with Hans, he pulled a line that opened a small valve in the top of the balloon. As hot air escaped we fell like a rock in a descent that might well have killed us all. It was a miracle we did not hit a mountain peak. Only when the balloon stabilized was Steve able to begin his attempt to resuscitate me.

A Breach Rebirth

Oblivious to his fight to save me, I felt unspeakable joy engulf every fiber of my being as I responded to a pull stronger than Earth's gravity. Once I was inside the tunnel it was as if someone at the other end was calling my name, drawing me forward. I knew that this passageway was taking me to the top of the mountain, leading me home into the Light. I was overjoyed to be going to the summit, as all my life I had wanted to climb to the top of Mt. Rainier. I had never made the attempt, believing that I would try and fail, or that I would die trying.

I moved effortlessly into the passage. Soon I knew I would be able to fly.

Fly?!

The Light was getting brighter and warmer as I moved through the tunnel. The MUSIC, the celestial symphony, continued to fill the air with a psalm of Oneness, played on unseen instruments of peace.

I arrived at the pinnacle and, standing at the entrance to the Light, took a single step, leaving my right footprint imbedded in Eternity. I entered a sacred space—a place where I knew I had returned to my most essential nature, where I felt wholly and consciously united with all things and Source, where a soothing balm of peace was poured on my spirit by an unseen hand, an emollient so rich in love that to this day I cannot fully absorb or comprehend it.

And then, in one ephemeral glimpse, I saw the Pattern, the single strand of the tapestry I knew was the essence woven through matter in every reality. Its design was so complexly simple that I knew it could only have been fashioned in the exalted intricacy of infinity.

Seeing the Pattern, I knew I was looking at life itself. It was light; it was time and space. It was the energy of all matter, the heart of all that mattered. It was the very essence of all being. It emanated from Source, illuminated to my mind by "the Source behind the sun" as it moved in perfect harmony with all the universe. As I prepared to meld into the Source of Light and absolute Love, I knew with all my being that the Pattern was the core of all substance. I knew that the MUSIC emanating from the Pattern was the song of my heart, a testament of unconditional Love. The single step I had taken was the first in a dance that would take me into the single point of Infinite Light, which contained the power of Love that would forever illuminate my mind and heart. I inhaled and prepared to take the next step as the exhalation of Love, the Life Force of the universe, carried me home, when, without warning, the melody screeched. Before I could move, a cacophony assaulted me. A cold wind rushed past me, and I remember crying out, "No!"

I knew I was in a life-or-death struggle, this time with an unknown adversary who had grabbed me by my left foot. I was struggling with an enemy who was attempting to yank me backward, pulling me away from the Light. I was enraged. I did not want to leave. Yet, even as I was being dragged back, I knew I had to remember. I twisted to the right to look at the Pattern, knowing I must not forget.

The enemy was my loving partner, Steve. As he frantically administered CPR, he pummeled my chest, forcing oxygen to circulate in my body. Later he would insist that as I reentered my body, my windmilling fists were empowered with an otherworldly rage.

The exact length of time I was "dead," in what is often referred to as a near-death experience, remains uncertain. However, making the ascent from twelve thousand feet, where I remember going out of my body, to more than seventeen thousand feet would probably have taken more than fifteen minutes.

From the point of being pulled back into and through the tunnel, I have virtually no memories. The next hours, days, weeks, and months are gone, save the memory of rage. For almost a year my life became a calendar without notations.

Blithe Spirit Hovering

Although we were now at a lower altitude, Hans was unable to raise anyone on the radio. Since he had no idea where we were, all he could do was search for a safe place to land. Three key elements were nonnegotiable in bringing the wayward airship back to earth: (1) a field large enough to deflate the balloon without damage, although at this point this was not a primary concern; (2) a road reasonably close so our chase crew could retrieve us; and finally, (3) telephone lines so we could notify race headquarters and our crew as to where we were.

As the winter sun set behind the mountains, the deepening shadows made it increasingly difficult to see. An already serious situation was compounded by the deteriorating weather and the disturbing fact that we were low on propane. Both men were also more fully realizing the gravity of my condition.

After what must have seemed an eternity, they spotted a field and frantically prepared to descend. Moments later we made a very rough landing when the wind caught our basket, tipped us over, and dragged us through a snowy, rock-filled pasture. Miraculously, no one was seriously hurt.

After digging out and securing the balloon, Steve and Hans carried me several hundred yards to the old farmhouse they had spotted from the air. Here, an elderly couple welcomed us into their home, giving us what Steve described as warm vinegar to drink.

Several hours passed before we were picked up, and only then was our miracle fully appreciated. We had landed less than a quarter of a kilometer from the Czechoslovakian border. Had Hans hesitated when landing for even a few moments, we certainly would have crossed that invisible line. Because hot air balloons had been used in recent years by individuals intent on freedom, it is likely that our fate would have been determined by overzealous border guards.

Although Steve was successful in reviving me, one thing was certain—the woman he had brought back was not the same one who had left. After learning that I was in essence a being of Light, I had to come back into this world and reenter a dense, physical body. Furthermore, almost every belief I had embraced only hours before—that I was a physical being, that love was outside of me, that God was some patriarchal monarch sitting on a marble throne somewhere in the sky, that death was something to fear, that I was doomed by my past, that religion and spirituality were the same, that spirituality and science were different—was no longer true to my experience. Virtually every picture of "reality" I had used to define my existence—not to be confused with my life—had been cremated. The ashes of the woman I thought I was were scattered on the wind.

CHAPTER FOUR

A Second Chance, a Conscious Choice

A Season of Rage

*L*ike the multi-impaired child Steve and I had seen only hours before, I was clearly brain damaged, though not as severely. All too quickly it became obvious that I had left more than my blithe spirit hovering over the Austrian Alps. I felt as if some vital substance that fueled my essence had spilled like oil on a roadway. It seemed that a large part of my psyche had stubbornly chosen to remain on the bridge over which I had crossed into Eternity.

Neither Steve nor I realized at the time how our lives would be permanently altered on that winter day. Erased were blocks of my long- and short-term memory. As a result I would be required to relive many segments of my life secondhand.

I had no idea that months and years of healing were just beginning. The physical repercussions from the hypoxic episode were the tip of the iceburg. I was enraged to find myself locked into a body that was supposed to know and do basic things, things that I could no longer figure out. I felt trapped inside an obsolete body with a defective brain that seethed with fear and anger. I was at the mercy of inner demons—the physical, spiritual, emotional, and psychic blackguards whom Death had left in its wake.

Three weeks following the accident I was given a second chance at this life, an opportunity to gather a handful of new strands and begin to reweave the fabric of my existence.

The question would be—did I want to?

On February 7, 1987, I woke up in the middle of the night, unable to figure out why Steve was sitting on the foot of our bed. More annoyed than curious, I was irate because his weight was binding the covers around my feet. Struggling to sit up, I switched on a small bedside lamp, noticing that the red digital numbers on the alarm clock glowed 1:14 A.M.

I turned, expecting to give Steve a piece of my mind (not that I had any to spare), but to my amazement saw that it was my father sitting there. He was as solid, as "real" as you are here and now holding this book. For reasons I cannot explain even now, this seemed the most natural thing in the world, even though almost ten years had passed since his death.

"How could you leave?" I asked. I could not comprehend why in Heaven or on Earth he would choose to leave where I knew he had come from.

My father told me that he had been "allowed"—this was the word he used—to return, which my brain interpreted to mean that he had somehow been permitted to appear in a physical form. He told me he was there to give me a gift of love and the remembrance of choice. I was being permitted to decide for myself whether to return to the Light or remain here on Earth. The choice was mine, and mine alone.

I clearly recall the inner dialogue and the lengthy but wordless communication I had with my father. Everything I needed to see to make the decision—past, present, and, to some degree, future—was placed in front of me. It wasn't as if I were getting to reshuffle the cards; it was as though I were being given a new deck. If I chose to play, I knew I was going to be required to play with the cards all face up. There was to be no bluffing.

Suddenly the picture of what was yet to be became exceedingly clear. I remembered what I had been told on the other side by the *presence*—that I would be a catalyst for change, for love. I knew with certainty that this had not yet begun.

In that moment, three influences affected my decision to stay: (1) the children, a thought that at the time I translated to mean my children; (2) the Pattern, which I had seen when I took my step beyond the tunnel, and which I knew I was supposed to remember, although it eluded me now; and (3), as nonrational as it seemed (both then and especially now), the *presence*. I wanted to meet this individual and had an unshakable sense of knowing that he was on this side waiting for me to figure it all out. Goddessence knew, and I wanted to figure out how it was that this stranger had shown up center stage in my life review. Even if he were an angel, a celestial guide, or a cosmic guardian of some sort, I decided that I wanted to be around if and when he showed up again. I had more than a few questions and figured he had more than a few answers. (To this day, I remain clueless about him.)

This may well have been the first time in my life that I didn't need someone else to tell me what to do. For once I knew what I needed, and perhaps more importantly, I knew what I wanted. I wanted to stay.

On that frigid, snowy morning I told Daddy I wanted to stay. When he told me how much he loved me, I wept, having never heard him say those words. I told him how much I loved him and how grateful I was he had returned to give me such a priceless gift.

I believe it was in this moment that I began the "progress of" (growth toward) extending forgiveness to both of us, most especially to myself—forgiveness for allowing his and others' beliefs to bind me in those Byzantine "thou shalt knots," forgiveness for not realizing that love is the reason I came to Earth in the first place, and forgiveness for doubting that I was worthy and deserving of love.

When I asked him to be my Guide and help me remember, he lovingly assured me that he, my grandmother, and others were always right beside me. He reminded me that all I had to do was ask for help.

With my decision made, Dad then left me with his final gift, the simple truth that I would never rediscover the Light of Love by analyzing the darkness. And then he turned and returned into the Light.

Even now I am warmed by the radiance of his Goddessential essence, the Light of Eternity that shone through his being.

Inside Out or Outside In?

Suddenly alone, I knew I had to find Steve and tell him what had happened. Still physically warm from the encounter with my dad and the nearness of the Light, I was immune to the chill penetrating the house. I got out of bed without even pausing to put on a robe or slippers. Struggling to maintain my balance, I went looking for him, making it only halfway down the hall outside of my daughter's bedroom door. Instinctively, I knew I was in trouble and, in a flash, entered a state of hyperconsciousness. I was jolted by the shock of what was happening. I was leaving my body. I was dying. As this knowing suffused my brain and body, I argued with God, thinking, "But I said no!"

Steve was in the family room reading when he heard me scream, "But I said no!"

Suddenly I was amazed to find myself suspended over the shower in the bathroom, looking down on my body. From this vantage point I was observing my death and the ensuing chaos in a most detached manner.

"How did my body get into the bathroom?" I wondered, as I saw my half-nude body lying on the floor. I recall thinking, "I didn't know the ceiling was this high," as the eight-foot ceiling felt like it was at least thirty feet high.

I no longer had any doubt that the body was just a shell, a temporary abode of a spiritual being. And at that moment I knew I was not "home."

More than fifteen minutes passed before my consciousness returned to the physical world. During the interim I had my second near-death experience, of which I have only one memory. I recall lying on my back on a hard, cold surface in a very dark space. Above me were what I would call threads of light, and I knew that I had to get out of my "body" as I experienced it there if I were going to get out of that dark space and back into my "real" body. I had an impression of where I was, but nothing that made rational sense. In those intervening moments between leaving my body and coming back as a silent, unseen witness, I somehow knew that I was inside the Great Pyramid. How I got there or why was beyond my understanding. I returned to this world with virtually no memory of the journey, nor do I have any recollection of seeing the tunnel again. It was obvious, however, that I had been somewhere else, once again crossing the great divide of dimensionality.

Below me, my body was now surrounded by four burly paramedics wearing yellow rain slickers, black pants, and huge snow-caked boots. They were dripping wet, making a ridiculous mess, and I found it quite comical to watch them crammed into this tiny room.

I also watched and listened as Steve, who harbored a profound contempt for paramedics, fought with them. He insisted that nothing they were doing was right. "Listen to me," he screamed, "I'm a doctor!"

I felt the tension build, and when the senior—and largest—medic's patience expired, I remember thinking, "Uh-oh. Steve's grace period is up."

I watched from my unique perspective as the medic stood up and physically assisted Steve out of the bathroom. He told him in no uncertain terms, "You may be a doctor, but I'm in charge! Now shut up, stay out of our way, and let us do our job."

Unfortunately, my daughter had a friend spending the night who that day had returned from her mother's funeral. As Julia stood in the hallway directly behind my head screaming "Now my mother's dead" over and over again, I desperately tried to communicate with her. I wanted to let her know I hadn't gone and would be right back. But my effort was to no avail. As her little friend sobbed in the corner, I also tried to communicate with her, to let her know her mom was fine. How I knew this was so, I have no idea, but I knew it was.

From my perch over the shower stall I watched every procedure the medics performed and heard every word of their radioed conversation with the doctors at the hospital. I listened as they told the emergency room physician, "We have a thirty-four-year-old white female. No pulse. No blood pressure. Respiration zero."

I remember laughing, thinking it was wonderful they thought I was thirty-four, because I had just turned thirty-five. Didn't they know that age and time had no real meaning anyway?

As they transported my body, I moved too, following as they transferred me—my body that is—to the ambulance. All the while I desperately tried to get Steve's attention, willing him to "look up." I wanted him to know that I was not in that body.

I watched his rage and frustration hit a new high when the exasperated medics would not let him ride in the ambulance, insisting that he follow them in his car. It was not a pretty sight as he then fought them for the right to have me taken to the hospital where he was on staff rather than the one closest to their station. This was the only battle he won that night.

I watched his rage escalate still further as he sat freezing in the car while the medics took their time preparing to transport. I was puzzled as they remained in the driveway for a long while. I watched while the medic in the back with me fiddled with the intravenous lines. I was curious when I saw him remove the oxygen mask from my face and furious when he turned to the driver and said, "Take it easy on the ice. They'll pronounce her D.O.A. at G.S.H."

I remember thinking, "You're in for one big surprise, buddy."

Only moments later my spirit reconnected with my body. I do not recall what, other than intention, propelled me, but I remember and can feel the exact sensation of "sliding" back into my body, going feet first through the top of my head like a baseball player sliding into home base. It was as if I started running, made a charge toward my body, and then slid through the top of my head. I accurately recall what I saw out both windows of the ambulance when I opened my eyes. It was incredible! Suddenly, I was back!

Then and there I understood what had happened. I had to die again to make my choice effective. I had to return to the other side, and from there make it my singular intention to come back. From wherever it was, I knew I had to leave the darkness to find the Light. Living had to be a self-empowered decision, a conscious act of my own volition. Once again, time had warped, cracked, and slipped out of sync.

I will never forget the look on the paramedic's face when I opened my eyes and said, "Hi." And I cannot tell you how many times I've wished I'd had the presence of mind to say, "Boo!"

We pulled into the emergency room driveway on two wheels, and all too clearly I recall the back doors flying open. Forever needle phobic, I watched in silent horror as a woman doctor lunged at me with a huge hypodermic in hand. When she grabbed my left wrist and slammed it deep, I screamed in pain. Needless to say, I gave her quite a shock— obviously not the D.O.A. she was expecting! She was drawing for arterial blood gases to pronounce the time of my death.

Later when the lab results were returned, they showed all my blood gases "flat." All systems had shut down and I had indeed "died." No one could account for what had happened. There did not seem to be a rational medical explanation for what caused me to "die," nor could anyone explain how I found my way back.

More significantly for me, no one wanted to hear from me about what had happened. Admitted to the hospital for extensive tests, I soon began to see anew how thoroughly scared and confused Steve was. We were both trapped. From this point on, I believe each of us slid deeper into our separate chaos. We spent the next five years struggling in vain to build a bridge across the chasm that separated us. Steve's mantra became, "I want the woman I first met. I want her back."

She never returned.

Practice Makes Perfect?

I left the hospital a scared and reluctant traveler, emotionally hesitant to embark on a long journey in which I was in control of neither the transportation nor my eventual destination. I could only pray that the pilgrimage of my soul would lead to remembrance and the restoration of my heart to w-holy-ness and my body to wellness.

I continued to be angry that I could not do many of the things we all take for granted—mundane things like verbally expressing myself in a lucid and intelligible manner, walking without losing my balance, and remembering what I had for lunch. I had a difficult time speaking a logical thought, forget trying to write one. Yet, at the same time I insisted—as best I could—that I had been "assigned to communication" and was supposed to write.

Uh-huh.

I was continually embarrassed when, in the middle of a sentence, the mental glue that was supposed to connect my thoughts simply deteriorated, and it all fell apart. I knew what I wanted to say, but the fuses in my brain blew when I tried to say it. So, too, repeatedly the simplest attempt to send a command to my foot or hand short-circuited as if the force of my intentions caused a power surge. I felt totally disconnected, lost in a dark and obscure space as I wandered very much alone in a mental, physical, and emotional blackout.

Eventually Steve and the other doctors determined why my crisis during the balloon ascent had been so severe, while neither he nor Hans had suffered any long-term problems. Apparently during my childhood bout with spinal meningitis I had suffered undiagnosed damage deep within my brain, an injury that had never before caused a problem. However, this obscure bruise was a cerebral time bomb. The combination of this prior injury, plus the long-term lack of oxygen, my extremely low blood pressure, my high blood alcohol (from the jaga tea the night before), and the high altitude pushed a button and made for one big explosion.

After months of countless therapies, C.A.T. scans, M.R.I.s, E.E.G.s, and every other test known to modern medicine, we finally wound up in the offices of an internationally known neurologist. He told Steve, "You have to change your life, because the woman you left with is not coming back. As you know, this kind of damage is permanent." He continued, "The chemistry in Lynnclaire's brain is such that I don't want her to drink water or take in any fluids unless her mouth is so dry she can't make saliva." Filling a sheaf of prescription pads, prescribing daily doses of everything from antiseizure drugs to antidepressants, he informed Steve, "She'll be on medication for the rest of her life. She shouldn't drive and can't fly. I don't want her on a stepladder above sea level unless she has oxygen. So, no more plane trips, and for heaven's sake, no more ballooning. She won't be able to tolerate stress of any kind."

Steve argued with him regarding fluid intake but was rebuffed and told to hire help for the house because we were going to need all the help we could get.

It was some time later that I overheard doctors discussing my most recent C.A.T. scans. "The area of the brain that appears the most damaged is ..." A closing door cut off the rest of the sentence, and I remain grateful that I never did learn the end of that conversation. I know that this type of information, once injected into the subconscious, often becomes a self-fulfilling prophecy.

My fears of not being good enough, of letting people down, and of being dependent were exacerbated by the fact that I could not reason anything out in a rational manner. Nothing made sense, and no matter how many times I dredged the abyss within myself I could not find a single clue as to who I was. To my bewilderment and others' dismay, I continued to be furious most of the time. Confusion compounded the fact that although a part of me had chosen to return, another part of me still did not want to be here.

On what was to me a virtually unexplainable level, I was tormented with far more than my obvious physical ailments. I suffered a grievous affliction of spirit. Although my body felt little pain, my mind and soul were in utter agony as I suffocated under a heavy cloak of rage. I questioned my every thought and mercilessly interrogated every feeling. Not a single day went by that I didn't both curse God and pray. I was powerless, invisible, voiceless, and hopelessly stuck.

I was terrified of what might be hiding under my anger. Doctors, Steve, and other well-meaning people brought my rage to the surface when they talked about me as if I weren't even there. Time and again I'd be sitting there and people would refer to me in the third person. My inner voice would scream, "I'm here, damn it! Talk to me, not about me."

Steve seemed not unwilling, but unable, to deal with the reality of our condition. I'm certain that he took my anger personally, feeling perhaps some remorse for having brought me back. My wrath was, I'm sure, a reflection of his pain, and I am sure also that there were times when he, too, wished he had not revived me.

All too clearly I recall the day two concerned neighbors came to visit. As they were leaving I overheard one say to the other, "Only six months together and now he's stuck with a lifetime of this. What a tragedy."

Devastating guilt now exponentially compounded my pain and anger.

Return to Paradise

As months passed I became progressively more shrouded in despair and sank into a deep depression. Countless times I asked myself why on earth I had wanted to come back. Then one day, as I was wrapped in my nearly impenetrable melancholy, a therapist challenged me. "You know, Lynnclaire, the average human being uses less than 10 percent of his or her brain, and you are far from average. Okay, maybe you did lose a big chunk of gray matter, but I think if you decided you really wanted to, you could call up replacement troops."

I remember thinking maybe he was right. I deeply respect those physicians and care givers who are true healers—those who realize that humans are more than bodies—and was coming to understand that there is a world of difference between curing what ails us and healing that which binds us. I had to move beyond the doctor's prognosis.

Seven months after the accident I met Steve at the front door to our home and told him, "I have to go to Mt. Rainier." In my heart, I knew if I were to ever fully live again, I had to make this trip. The mountain was an important spiritual place for me, and I felt that if I went there, I had a greater chance of finding my way to the next stage of my life. Maybe I could even find the other doorway. If I did, hopefully I would be able to get back to this side without being pulled through the keyhole.

Two weeks later, two girlfriends and I pulled out of the driveway in our motor home, off on a journey halfway across the country. Steve, who had serious misgivings but knew better than to argue, made plans to join me in Washington the following week.

Before we drove away I turned to him and said, "All I'm asking for is one day. This isn't a life worth living. I want one day with no pills, no therapy, no doctors, and no doubts. I can't deal with any more E.E.G.s, M.R.I.s, and C.A.T. scans. I pray I never have to see the inside of a doctor's office again. All I want is one day where I can feel. One day where I'm not in this fog. Then, and only then, will I be ready to die. Or live."

Five days later, as I was walking through the alpine meadows of Mt. Rainier, where the summer wildflowers were in full bloom, memories washed over my soul. As I walked in silence, I heard the MUSIC echoing through the valleys. Although I walked alone in body, I felt attended to by the spirits of my father and grandmother. There on my mountain I heard the echo of a child's whisper carried on the wind, "Where's my ocean?" And I heard another, vaguely familiar voice reply, "Wait for the waiting to be full."

That afternoon I flushed hundreds of dollars' worth of drugs down the toilet. When the sun set, I released my doubts and fears with it, resolving in that moment to reclaim my life.

CHAPTER FIVE

The Karmic Laundromat

Hot Wash, Cold Rinse

Almost two years later I found my-
self looking back, realizing that although I had defied the doctor's mental
and physical prognosis, there was a kind of spiritual cover-up going on.
Nothing I'd done had made me feel whole, let alone clean. What I wanted
was to feel and be the Light.

Instead, I still felt trapped, locked in emotional solitary confine-
ment, held hostage by my ever-attendant pain. I felt destined to be ban-
ished from joy as Steve and I struggled in our chaotic relationship, even
as I searched for the elusive Pattern I continued to believe contained
the answers I sought. But all I saw were old structures I knew all too
well—addictions of pain, denial, rage, and rejection. Although I was
still obsessed by what had happened in my near-death experience, a
naggy little voice inside insisted that my decision to come back into a
body had been ill advised. Unfortunately, there was no one to blame
but myself. I had made the decision entirely on my own.

As the skirmish in my brain raged, Steve—a genuine, can-do, positive-thinking kind of guy—exerted as much pressure as possible to get the "old" me back. Locked into the old paradigm of wanting to please, I spent an inordinate amount of time trying to be that woman. I invested my considerable energy in making his dreams come true and in attempting to disregard and forget the purpose I had been given. In spite of what I knew in my head, my heart was still not ready to let go of the old lie that if *he* was happy, *we* could be happy.

I soon realized that both Steve and I had whitewashed our experiences and denied our feelings, believing that at some essential level we had been permanently stained and that there was no way we could make love real. Consequently, it didn't take me long to reach a point where my depression was so deep, so dark, that I once again wanted to die. I knew if I couldn't turn it around soon then there was no point in going any further.

I was about to go through the wringer of change. It was to be a hot-water wash, and making it through was going to mean being willing to go through all the cycles.

The change began in July of 1988, when we relocated to California. Here Steve was finally going to fulfill his lifelong dream by establishing a West Coast medical practice. However, his long- and well-entrenched surgical business in the Midwest still was going to require his presence two weeks a month for some time.

The week before Christmas, our world collapsed around us with two emotionally calamitous events. First, we found out that the doctor whose California practice Steve was purchasing had been indicted on multiple counts of Medicare fraud. Every dollar of cash and sweat equity invested was at risk, and our attorney advised us to get out immediately. Second, my daughter arrived home from school for winter recess and told me she had a problem.

Dear God, I wondered, *what else?* The problem was not a small one. It was bulimia. The *good news* was she told me and wanted help.

Within twenty-four hours she was admitted to a residential eating-disorder hospital, and only days later we moved again, this time to a beach community near San Diego. Even though the time together in Steve's and my long-distance relationship was soon to get longer, we were not destined to get closer together. Especially because neither of us was willing to return to the Midwest.

The Spin Cycle

Although I would never have admitted it, I was spending far more time than I even now care to admit contemplating the how-to's of dying. In retrospect I remain grateful there was a piece of me that was still completely obsessed with what other people thought, a part of me that couldn't bear thinking of the shame that would accrue if I dared to change my mind and take an early checkout. I was so emotionally exhausted that I was now sure there was nothing to live for.

I know that I survived this time only because of the untold hours I spent with my best friend, Lael. Together we tried to piece the fragments together, talking about life and the elusive Pattern. She patiently listened to what little I remembered, heard what I was feeling, and on some level seemed to know and understand what I was talking about even though it was totally nonrational.* Countless times it seemed her kitchen stools had cosmic rocket launchers attached to the legs, as we blasted off into a deep inner space.

"It feels like this," I would say, drawing spirals and tunnels up and down. "But it also feels like hearts," I'd mutter as I scribbled, drawing intricate honeycombs, eights, and cubes. "But how can a circle be a square be a heart be a pyramid be a rectangle?" I asked, as I drew stars, diamonds, spiderwebs, crescents, circles, and crosses. How could they, too, be the same?

* Nonrational is not synonymous with irrational—it merely defines that which falls outside whatever can be logically explained.

But no matter how hard I thought, no matter how strongly we willed those deleted pieces of my brain to come back for an encore, we could not find, nor could I remember, the Pattern. I wanted to remember, thinking that if I remembered I wouldn't have to be afraid. I did not realize then that until I was no longer afraid, there was no way I could remember. I knew there was more to life, but I had no idea how to find it and had all but abandoned the hope that the elusive something that would make me happy was "out there." I never dreamed it could be lurking anywhere inside of me.

Meanwhile, my daughter's bulimia had me perplexed. I was convinced it was some contagious disease kids were infected with at school. Perhaps my daughter's pediatrician had forgotten to give her some childhood vaccination that would have rendered her insusceptible. This disease seemed to be epidemic, the teenage malady *du jour*.

Nevertheless, for two months I showed up at the hospital twice a week to participate in the family therapy program. Like many of the other parents, I quickly came to the bleak conclusion that parenting is the last bastion of the amateur. Having long thought of myself as a failure at motherhood, I thought for sure this would be my emotional Waterloo. However, I decided that since I was already on my way down, I might as well go down fighting. What a fight it turned out to be.

So, while Julia was slogging through her issues, I was slugging it out with the shrinks. You see, these therapists seemed thoroughly persuaded that I had a major problem as well—one that was decidedly worse than anorexia or bulimia, to hear them tell it. What's more, it seemed that I was presenting nothing less than the classic, final-stage symptoms of this fatal malady called "codependency." I could not believe they actually had the audacity to tell me that not only was this supposed disease going to kill me, but it was going to do so ten times faster than gorging and gagging would ever kill someone with bulimia.

Even though I kept telling them I was there for my daughter—*vol-*

untarily no less—they insisted that I had better change my mind and show up for myself. Why? "Because," they insisted, "you are sicker than your kid."

The first time they said this my knee jerked and my mouth flew open. "Get out of here," I railed.

I had to believe that this codependency business was all psychological gobbledygook. I was as normal as members of this species come—even if I did spend a lot of time trying to figure out what on earth "normal" was. My relationships were as functional as anyone else's were, even though I was miserable much of the time. So what if when you were sick I took care of you, cooked your meals, cleaned your house, and schlepped your kids to gymnastics, but when I was sick chose not to tell you? I could take care of myself. Well, if that was a disease, it must be the result of some biological accident of birth, the consequence of being conceived in a shallow psychic and emotional gene pool. They, too, discounted my near-death experience and didn't want to hear about it and didn't seem to think dying counted for anything. All I knew for certain was that although my near-death experience had certainly changed some of my attitudes about life, the experience hadn't yet sprouted me a pair of wings. I soon saw that there was no way I could fly over the compost heap known as my past *and* present. So, it seemed that the safest thing to do was just plug my nose and try to walk around it. If that didn't work, no doubt sooner or later I'd wind up buried alive under it. Now *here* was a pattern even I could see.

As the days wore on—and on, and on, and endlessly on—I was forced to examine many of the hideous wounds to my soul, not to mention the ones I'd inflicted on my child. I also saw that we both still had quite a few fresh scabs on our spirits and psyches. I, too, was beginning to believe that this codependency condition might indeed be fatal. What's worse, it looked to be a much more painful death than the two I had already experienced.

During a particularly confrontational Thursday night session I was again the solo target in front of this firing squad of therapists. That night I decided I could not and would not take any more.

"Just one %#^$&# minute," I screamed through my tears. "If I'm the one who is so sick, how come my daughter is the one in a hospital?" Undaunted and truly bewildered, I continued. "How come there's a Betty Ford Center for my mom and this place for my kid? If I'm so sick, messed up, and walking dead to hear you tell it, why isn't there some place for me to go? I seem to have a black belt, maybe even a Ph.D., in this disease you call codependency. So how come there's no hospital for me?"

To look at the therapists' faces you would never have known how angry and desperate I was. Virtual paragons of patience, they merely looked at me, smiled, and I believe sincerely murmured, "Thanks for sharing, Lynnclaire. Keep coming back."

With a calm far more dangerous than my fury, I replied, "I'm sick and tired of coming here on Thursday and letting you beat me until I am a bloody pulp. I go home for five days, come back, and all you do is pull off the scabs. What's more, you don't even offer me a Band-Aid. Haven't I bled enough?"

Ranting as I stormed out that night, I announced that I was going to go and visit my friends Mr. Baskin, Mr. Robbins, and Mrs. Fields. My parting shot was that if anyone wanted to join me, I was buying. I'm ashamed to say that two hours later Domino's attempted to deliver a half dozen (prepaid, of course) pepperoni pizzas to the eating-disorder unit, where food was strictly portioned, and junk food of any kind was forbidden.

I was suicidal, as terrified and mad as I had ever been in my life. However, for once my anger saved a life—mine.

Baby Food and Baby Talk

It was only days later, on February 24, 1989, that I found the rusty key that unlocked the door to my prison cell. Within hours I would begin to emerge from the darkness, making another 180-degree turn—this time toward a ray of hope.

Several weeks before, Steve, an alumnus of virtually every eighties-type human-potential workshop, signed us up for a weekend seminar with the latest guru to hit the psychospiritual self-help circuit.

However, I, for one, was not interested. Granted, if one believed all the hype, this new guru was on the emotional fast track, but I'd been running in that rut too long. After weeks of sitting though regurgitation at the eating-disorder hospital, I was not the least bit interested in a fancy heap of psychological health food.

No, no way. This event was definitely not for me. I'd already spent most of my lifetime exercising and "shaping up," doing every kind of mental gymnastics. I was an expert at emotional aerobics, a certified master at jumping to conclusions, not to mention a card-carrying member of the "toeing-the-line club."

No. I was not interested in doing any weekend workshop, and the more I thought about it, the stronger my resistance became. By this time almost every part of me had abandoned hope. I had all but given up remembering the moments when I had walked on the other side. Now all I longed for was to go "home," and the only way I knew to get there was to die. As much as I wanted to remember, I also wanted to forget the purpose, the warmth, the Light, the peace, and, yes, the *presence.*

So why bother with some lecture?

But in spite of my resistance, Steve prevailed, telling me that, as he had prepaid the workshop, we *were* going.

Armored: That's Not Amoré

Hauled into what I thought would be a two-day lecture on my daughter's problem, I soon realized I'd been set up. It was only after we arrived that I was informed that this rehabilitated reverend's weekend discourse was entitled "Healing Abandonment and Rejection."

I knew I'd never get out of there alive.

That night, along with two thousand other sitting ducks—a smattering of skeptics interspersed with a multitude of believers—I found myself in the middle of something akin to a tent meeting. I was about to discover that this was nothing less than a crash course in emotional growth. By the end of the evening I'd have wagered my soul that most of the people who were there had absolutely no idea how they got there—in the building, not to mention grown up.

By default—Steve's fault—I discovered that I was registered in emotional kindergarten, led by a teacher who was a specialist at removing pacifiers and a master at divesting one of all artificial identities.

S.O.S.: Sick of Suffering

In his book *The Passionate Life*, Sam Keen says, "So, with gratitude and anger we leave childhood behind, and limping we proceed on our journey towards wholeness."

Well, my psyche was definitely hobbling that Friday night, but I would finally begin to inch toward wellness and remembrance.

That night resurrected the memories of the mountain, awakened me again to the truth that there *was* a child living within my being. Her name was "Sissy," and she was a five-year-old magical child who was very much alive and in incredible pain.

That night my pain was named and I was thoroughly exposed, my most logical rationales unraveled. I didn't know whether to bless the seminar leader or curse him, as the piece of me who was an emotional toddler sat in the ballroom "crib" that evening.

However, I still had my security blanket clutched firmly in one hand, with the thumb of my other jammed tightly in my mouth. No way was I going to come back tomorrow and talk. I'd learned at the eating-disorder hospital that this sharing stuff was painful. Besides, hadn't I always been told, "Good little girls don't ever talk to strangers," "Children do not speak unless they're spoken to," and "Big girls don't cry"? The rules in my family stated clearly that when I left the house, everything that happened there *stayed* there.

Nevertheless, I knew that my inner sanctuary was a haunted house filled with skeletons rattling behind every closed door.

The adult in me had been at a total loss as to how to protect my innocent, childlike self. Unable to find a safe place, I had erected high and thick walls of separation. These barriers made communication, especially between Steve and me, impossible. But that night truth hollered so loud that I heard in spite of my walls.

I wasn't sure, however, if I had what it would take to be able to scream loud enough to ask for help.

I knew that if I talked I'd be opening Pandora's box, and there was no way I'd ever be able to get the lid back on. No way was I coming back Saturday morning.

Then the miracle happened when a man stood behind the podium and threw me a life ring.

Was I hearing things, or did he really say something about an *inpatient* treatment center for codependency?

For weeks I'd been *begging* for help, asking for such a place, and had been led to believe that no such place existed.

Immediately I turned to Steve and asked him for a quarter. I flipped it in the air, said "Who goes first?" and asked him to call out heads or tails. "Heads," he said.

It was heads, but I was desperate. "Tails. I go first." I then used the quarter to make a phone call to the treatment center that had been mentioned, arranging to travel there Monday morning for an admissions interview.

Forty-eight hours after the workshop ended, I checked into a fledgling residential treatment center for codependency—located in, of all

places, Hollywood, California. Little did I imagine that, in the city famous for creating illusion, all my fantasies would break down. Never
could I have imagined that, in the land of bright lights and tinsel, I
would have to face my worst nightmares with all the lights on. However, I knew that if I had any hope of seeing a new way of being, and of
remembering what I had forgotten, this was it.

Childhood: A Second Time Around

When I went for a preliminary intake appointment, I was told the
first thing on the admissions agenda was completing an "Identified Patient Evaluation form." I panicked. Was this a *test?* Was it multiple-choice
or essay? Was it a pass-fail exam? What if they determined there was
nothing wrong with me? What if they rejected me?

No way. They were ecstatic! The *perfect* patient had arrived! "Well,
what do you know," I thought. "For once in my life I got something
right." They assured me I had all the proper credentials.

Their belief was confirmed the following day when I arrived with
my silk pillow shams, eiderdown comforter, new satin pajamas (matching robe and mule slippers, of course), three baskets of African violets,
a menagerie of stuffed animals, a dozen candles, incense, my personal
monogrammed bath towels, and white wicker bed tray.

Later they admitted that they could hardly wait to see *who* was going to check out five weeks later.

I knew it was time to get to work. To both my therapists' chagrin,
they promptly discovered that my mouth was no longer in neutral. I
was in high gear for healing and determined to let them prove that
their center was the shame-free zone they said it was. Miraculously, I
managed to give up virtually all my fears, especially my dread of embarrassment. Here, there were no roles to play, no rules to obey, and the
only expectations I had to fulfill were my own. I knew I had a major job
to do, and so promptly became my own worst taskmaster.

My first morning in group, the therapists congratulated me on my courage to come in and do this work and asked me what I was feeling. I had no idea what they were talking about or what they wanted from me. They didn't want to hear what I thought, they wanted to know how I felt. Until they put me in front of a chart with a couple dozen faces and the emotion each was supposed to reflect, I was clueless.

Okay. "I guess I'm scared. Enthusiastic. Sad. Safe." They applauded. "Whew," I thought, "I guess I passed."

They then went on to inform me that as the "old" me died, the real me would be freed to become the new woman I wanted to be.

Died? Death? Who said anything about death and dying? This was *not* what I wanted to hear. However, I also now knew I was thoroughly confused, frightened past the point of numbness, and mad enough at Steve to stay out of sheer spite.

In retrospect I can admit, too, that at the time I was too daft to run before the doors closed and locked behind me. Small wonder Lael still talks about the day I *incarcerated* myself.

The weekend workshop had let me know that this was not going to be a month of fun in the sun. Before the first day was over, I also knew that it was not in any way going to be a sentimental journey. I quickly realized they would be using a series of emotional jackhammers to break me out of my concretized thinking so I could finally find my feelings.

Within hours I confirmed my long-held suspicion that hell is not some abysmal otherworldly pit of fire and brimstone located deep in the bowels of the universe. I had irrefutable evidence that it's right here on earth. It's a place a lot of us know very well—it's the cesspool called GUILT.

Gently, the staff let me know that, yes, I was in the infernal throes of pain and change, but it didn't mean I had to stay in the land of damnation. That was, of course, unless I *decided* the land of blame, shame, and make-believe was going to be my permanent home. No, thanks. I'd been there long enough.

It didn't take long to see that I had to give up my illusion of power and my delusion about being a *human-being-in-control.* "No problem," I thought, as I surrendered to the process that I prayed would become progress. I knew my life was definitely out of control and figured that if I gave up having to be in charge, at least it meant I couldn't be blamed if things went wrong.

Even as the bottom fell out, I almost immediately felt solid emotional ground under my feet. Although I was emotionally naked and barely conscious, I was, thank Goddessence, alive and waking up.

Down the Habit Hole

Soon I realized that I had survived; I had passed the past. I even saw that my ability to persevere represented a substantial level of accomplishment. I knew that the old tapes inside my head, the ones that droned on and on, filled with other people's old mantras—*If you don't do it my way, you'll never amount to anything. Who do you think you are? Special?* and *It's all your fault*—would stop playing by the time we were through.

But this meant I had to figure out how to shut off that damnable tape recorder. My father's tapes were the worst, in spite of our healing. If I were to make new life resolutions, I had to be willing to turn that infernal tape recorder off. I knew that only then would I free both of us to grow. At the deepest level of my being I knew this would mean I would have a chance to grow up and grow old as well. As exciting and novel an idea as this was, it was also terrifying.

I'll never forget when I realized why it is that so few of us recognize our own voice on audiotape when we hear it for the first time. Although I know this actually has mostly to do with acoustics of the head, I couldn't help but wonder if perhaps it doesn't also involve the heart. Maybe it's because since childhood so many of us have been conditioned to pay attention only to others' voices, thoughts, and ideas. Small wonder we don't recognize our own voices, let alone our own truths.

I figured out that the first step was to find the volume control on that reel-to-*real* contrivance and turn down the sounds of these old messages. Locating the on-off button, let alone unplugging this con-*trap*-tion, would take a while.

At the treatment center I began the second phase of the great adventure I had started two years before. In the preceding months I had managed to reclaim my brain and body against all odds, and I knew this was the chance to heal emotionally. Getting to the core of the matter, and figuring out what was the matter and what mattered, was frightening beyond measure. It meant making a journey into the void—the unknown, that ghastly place I had avoided for decades. Here, in my descent into the screaming silence, someone was forever telling me to breathe. Inhale. Exhale. Inhale. Exhale. I remembered that when I was giving birth to my children it was the rigorous monitoring of my breath that moved me safely through the depths of the pain.

As the six other patients told their stories, I discovered that my feelings were not serious character flaws and my secrets were not exceptional—they were universal. Furthermore, I discovered I was not the only one who'd bought into other people's belief systems.

Although my memories were somewhat tattered, my pain remained 100 percent intact. Soon I learned that the pain was good news, that at least I could feel something. As paradoxical as it seemed, they told me that if I could feel anything, especially my anger and pain, then there was hope that one day I'd also be able to feel love and joy.

The five weeks that I was at the treatment center, I listened to, heard, and finally honored the many voices within my being—my voices. As the pieces of me became stronger, they grew louder and more insistent. I learned to pay attention to my knowing and regularly checked in to hear what my inner voices had to say.

Incredibly, day by day, I unearthed new clues that supported my choice to come back. So, too, as I began to unravel the old patterns of my life, I began to believe that one day I would remember the Pattern.

I also began to break out of the antiquated molds that I had allowed others to put me into. I concluded that I was the only one who could free my soul from bondage and freely bond with another.

As spring emerged, a real piece of me began to bloom as my spirit opened in the light of unconditional acceptance. As truth unveiled my fears, I could now look people in the eye. There was a new tone in my voice. I saw that I was learning a new language, the language of forgiveness and unconditional love. My brain had finally surrendered and was willing to be of service to my heart; my essence had, to a much greater degree, merged with my spirit; but most important, my soul knew it was finally safe to return home.

In time I came to see myself as a *recovered* codependent; a *recovered* adult child of alcoholics. I realized that if I invested my energy in the belief that I was *recovering*, then I was sending others and myself the message that I was sick. Wellness and wholeness were states I could achieve only on my own. I was free to choose moment by moment, day by day. The only thing I was sick of was suffering.

I saw how in childhood I was infected with a disease now called codependency. It is a scourge that pollutes the psyche and spirit and thrives on the shame and blame that devour one's Goddessential selfhood. It germinates in the dark places of the brain where we are harassed by thoughts that we are not worthy of joy; we do not deserve abundance; we will never be able to do enough to merit blessings or love.

I, like others, am living proof that we can recover from this disease. It took me decades and death to remember that only from a loving place of being would I ever be able to live or love intentionally. Codependency had left me believing that I had to fight to win approval. It made my life a constant battleground where someone was always destined to lose or die. Relationships were gruesome war zones where intimacy was synonymous with infirmity.

Codependency did not entitle me or anyone else to claim a cure through the assignment of blame. Neither did I for one moment believe this was a disease intentionally passed to me by my parents. I adore them and honor that they, too, survived as best they could. Whatever neglect or lack of nurturing I felt was neither intentional nor the consequence of malicious ignorance. I knew that whatever memories of abuse that were held by the five-year-old in me—Sissy—were not necessarily reliable thirty years after the fact. But that didn't mean I shouldn't listen to and honor that piece of me and celebrate the fact that the part of me who was innocent and knew how to play was still alive!

My coping patterns sprouted and took firm root in the lie that most of us were told in our childhood—that we should *forgive and forget.* The truth was that although I forgave, I *never* forgot. Thus I grew up thinking that my inability to mentally or emotionally release my accumulating hurts was a serious character defect. As a result, shame became the hard-driving force behind my feelings of guilt, preventing my remembrance of what was real.

Fear kept me from seeing who I was and who I might become. I did not know how to be honest, open, and willing, and could never say, "I feel sad," "I feel mad," "I feel happy," or "I feel scared." All I had learned to utter was, "I feel *you* (followed by an accusation)." It would take me a long while to learn that these three words are *not* a feeling—they are the precursor to an indictment, one that is predicated upon the condemnation and humiliation of another.

I had often heard the adage, "It's never too late to have a happy childhood," and had long yearned to have a *play*-mate, a partner who wanted to share in a healthy, happy, fun, and loving relationship. My healing only came as I was willing to live that childhood a second time.

Even then there was no doubt in my mind that the bug of codependency would always be with me. I knew that if I made inappropriate choices they would empower that germ to make me relationsick again. However, I saw that every moment I'm given is a choice point. The choice is always mine whether to live in joy or to volunteer to be a victim. I am either on purpose, or I am not. I discovered that joy is not merely a smiley, happy face; rather it is the freedom to choose wellness and wholeness in every experience by finding the highest meaning. Joy comes when I am confident and willing to express here and now whatever I'm feeling in lovingly appropriate ways.

CHAPTER SIX

Homeward Bound

Happy Endings or Ending Happy?

*E*ven after five weeks at the treatment center, I still had hope for Steve and me. We had invested more than two years of our lives in our relationship, and as I was committed to finishing business, I vowed to stay. I was determined that we would realize a positive dividend on our efforts.

As I prepared to leave the center, I was unable to see that there was still a piece of myself that was stubbornly determined *not* just to get it right, but to get it *perfect.*

When I was discharged, the majority of the potpourri who made up "me" truly believed that Steve and I could have a relationship with a happy ending.

Following my going-away lunch, I carried my luggage, paraphernalia, and now expanded menagerie of stuffed animals to the entrance lobby. There I met Steve for only the second time in five weeks. He had his suitcase in hand, and as part of our deal, was ready to check in.

In spite of all that had happened in the past weeks we did not have much to say. I knew that he felt the same terror I'd felt weeks before. He had not participated in family therapy while I was at the center because he was now working full time in the Midwest. During these weeks I had found the answers for and about myself, but had not yet addressed the burning questions about us.

The new emotional boundaries I had established regarding safety mandated that I quickly leave the treatment center and not engage in any long conversation with him. Thus, we talked only briefly before he handed me the car keys and went to meet with the director for his intake evaluation.

Although I was still alone, I finally knew I was whole all by myself.

My new "family" escorted me to the parking lot, where we had a tearful farewell and made promises to stay in touch. As I started the car, the five people who knew me better than anyone else on the planet went back inside the facility.

I was struck with the realization that I was totally alone for the first time in weeks. This hit me like a bolt out of the blue, and left me with a mild psychic concussion. I realized I was free.

My healing had gone way beyond process to incredible *progress*. My therapists and I agreed that I had recovered the most essential pieces of my wholeness. My spirit was soaring! As I looked back at the walls of the treatment center through my rearview mirror, gratitude filled my heart. Behind those walls virtually all the obstacles blocking my path had been bulldozed, the boulders I'd carried on my shoulders pulverized into sand. The sticks and stones I'd carried to protect myself from mental adversaries and emotional adversities were now loam filling the rut I'd been stuck in for years.

Yet, as I sat in the idling car, I felt inexplicably distressed. Why was I scared? Then it dawned on me—I didn't feel old enough to drive! I burst out laughing, realizing that I had been so wrapped up in "inner child" work that I felt like a prepubescent juvenile stealing my parents' car! Instantly, I knew the task at hand was to make sure that the most grown-up part of my personality was sitting behind the wheel!

With exceeding caution, I pulled out of the parking lot and merged into traffic, diligently, I might add, avoiding the fast lane. After being multidimensionally nursemaided for more than a month, I was struck by the tempo of life beyond the wall. The amplitude of noise and the vortex of energy that swirled in Los Angeles were overwhelming. Two blocks from the center I felt as if I were about to be sucked up. Bombarded by stimulation I could not control, my mind set off in pursuit of the familiar. I turned on the radio for the first time in five weeks, only to be stunned at the relentless cadence of the rhythm. I found the rapid-fire staccato of the disc jockey's banter disconcerting. No wonder I never had a chance to listen to myself and hear those wee small inner voices. They only whisper; how could they ever be heard above such a din? Could I pay attention and safely drive amid all that noise? I didn't think so and turned off the radio.

As I entered the freeway on-ramp I had a vivid flash of understanding. Suddenly I knew why people discharged from a hospital are required to exit in a wheelchair, and why someone else is required to drive them home. Thankfully, I had to drive only thirty miles to Thousand Oaks. I was going to spend the weekend debriefing with Lael and do some serious reality checking.

If I had a prayer for every sentient being, it would be that they had a friend like Lael. She is the kind of friend who, if you get *one* in your lifetime, you know you have been truly blessed with wealth beyond measure. Lael redefines sisterhood and *real* family for me. The first day we met—remembered each other—she let me know that her heart, kitchen stool, and guest room were always open to me. Seven years later, whenever she gets an itchy dialing digit, she calls. She lets me know I'm on her mind at the drop of a thought.

During the long dark nights of my soul, Lael was my full moon. She was the one person who never doubted what was real for me. We were emotional and psychic buoys for one another. Both of our histories had gouged gorges in our self-esteem, chasms that rivaled the Grand Canyon. Although we were both caught up in the rushing rivers of doing, our feelings had been dammed up decades before, so that now only a trickle of hope flowed in the bottoms of our hearts.

That weekend we relived the hours, days, and weeks that I'd spent at the treatment center. Lael's partner, Jon, a paragon of patience, listened as we carried on. We went through every event like police investigators, looking for and examining every fiber and shred of evidence that had been left on my body and brain. Lael admitted that if I was *nuts* they may as well come and take us away together. We knew that although our unique ability to make wisecracks would no longer hide our pain, it would be our sense of humor that kept us alive.

As I sat at Lael and Jon's kitchen counter, I continued my struggle to remember the Pattern. In light of all this new information, and having disposed of so many dysfunctional patterns, we thought for sure a healthy one would certainly pop to the surface of my brain. It didn't. But not because we weren't making every possible human effort to coax it up.

Bonding, or Ties That Bind

Soon after Steve and I met, a friend of mine remarked, "Who's the thunder and who's the lightning?" It wasn't a question so much as it was an observation. However, since the balloon incident, our personal lives had taken on a decidedly different tonality, one that grew even more pronounced following stopovers at the treatment center.

During Steve's time at the center, the doctors persuaded him that he would experience a more satisfying life if he came down to earth and got in touch with his feelings. He decided it was worth a try. Within a matter of weeks I was living with someone I had never met, an experience that gave me a new understanding of how he felt with and about the "new me."

However, with his system not quite so revved, hope was renewed. Maybe we could get this relationship right. Despite the fact that neither of us was blissfully happy, we persevered, striving to maintain the status quo.

Because it seemed things were starting to smooth out, we decided to finally get married.

Three years after our first scheduled wedding we put the plans into action. Only this time there would not be hundreds of guests, an elaborate ceremony, nor a dash across the Alps. Instead we chose to have an intimate ceremony with only our children and three friends present.

Intimate Relationsick

Four months after our wedding Steve abandoned the doctors' directives and opted to go back to full speed ahead. Because I couldn't keep up and didn't even want to, we suffered a relapse and fell out of "elationship." Once again we began to experience toxic relationsick.

That spring, as our fantasy began to melt, I saw that the whiteness of hope had only been the glare of illusion. I had been blinded to the underlying truth.

That April, Lael and Jon were married and asked Steve and me to join them on their honeymoon to Kaua'i. But by the time we arrived on this lush paradise island, I felt forced to share my bed with my intimate companion of abandonment. I felt stranded, essensually alone on a rock that Mother Nature had burped up in the middle of the Pacific Ocean.

By the end of the trip, I had allowed myself to be squeezed back into the form Steve had previously designed for me to wear. For the next year I modeled the wardrobe he created for me—the one that fit his picture of who *he* was and how I looked next to him. I again worked to make his dream happen. But even though I was doing it, this time I was doing it differently.

CHAPTER SEVEN

Genesis of Remembrance

A Ring of Fire

$\mathcal{W}$e returned to the mainland, and three months later made another trip to Hawai'i, this time on a combination of pleasure and business. As we prepared to return home, an unexpected business opportunity arose that required my staying in the islands for several extra days. While seeing Steve and the kids off to the mainland, my son Ryan asked, "Mom, you aren't moving to Hawai'i, are you?"

I looked him in the eye and in all honesty answered, "Are you nuts? No way. I'd never want to live on a rock in the middle of the ocean."

Nothing was farther from my mind or interested me less. Hawai'i was a great place to visit but definitely not someplace I'd choose to live. I remembered all too well my mother's feelings about living in the islands. In the early seventies, she and my dad came to Maui for a holiday, and once Daddy got his feet in the sand he knew he'd never leave. I'd spent the next several summers there with them and during these

75

interludes fully determined that they—Daddy, anyway—had gone over the edge. Mother hated it, and I clearly remembered her going on and on about "Rock Fever." What's more, I still had a vivid recollection of the one-way ticket Dad had thumbtacked to the bulletin board—hers to use anytime she wanted. But everyone knew he was staying.

Me move to Hawai'i? *No way.* I assured my son that I'd be home in two days.

The following morning, August 7, 1990, I boarded a flight in Līhu'e, Kaua'i, bound for Kailua-Kona on the big island of Hawai'i (commonly known as the Big Island).

That day paradise was shrouded in clouds as a tropical weather system pushed across the entire state. As torrential rains fell on the already drenched, humid island of Kaua'i, I prayed Kailua-Kona would be dry.

We lifted into ominous cumulous clouds and within minutes encountered heavy turbulence. It was as if the omnipresent Hawaiian deities were tossing the plane around like a cosmic beach ball. The constant upheaval kept everyone down, with the captain requiring all seat belts to be pulled snug.

The only thing I enjoyed that morning was my conversation with the flight attendant, a young woman who was also restricted to her jump seat. She was a *kama'āina* (local), born and raised on the island of O'ahu. I found it unimaginable that at the age of twenty-four she had *just* returned from her first trip to the U.S. mainland. I was further astounded when she asserted that she did not care to ever return. It was incomprehensible to me what it was that she, my dad, and others found so special about Hawai'i.

"What about Rock Fever?" I asked, again recalling that one-way eastbound ticket tacked up in my parents' kitchen.

"Hawai'i is in the heart," she replied.

Okay . . . Although I still didn't get it, I was envious of her strong sense of belonging. For years I had felt rootless. For as long as I could remember, I had desired a sense of belonging to a place where I knew I was *safe;* where I would feel loved, cherished, and protected. For years I'd prayed for such a haven, a place where in my heart of hearts I knew I would always be welcome. The only place I'd ever touched this knowing was on "the other side," but I hadn't given up finding it on Earth.

Still, it was amazing to me that anyone could send such deep roots through the lava into this small cluster of oversized pebbles. There was no way I could possibly imagine being content stranded on a tremor-prone boulder in the middle of the deep blue sea.

As I looked out the window, my thoughts took me again to the trip I had made to the other side of the cosmos, to a place near the Source behind the sun. I *knew* that home was in there, out there, or up there—wherever *there* was. Yet I also *knew* in my soul that home was a place *within* myself.

Looking out on the heavens I knew I was back on the planet for a reason. What's more, like it or not, I remembered the purpose I had been given. Now if I could only remember *how* to accomplish it. Finding all kinds of designs in the clouds, I once again found the word *pattern* presenting itself in my brain. As always, even two-and-a-half years after the accident, I had a pencil at hand, ready to remember, but I kept drawing a blank.

Nothing was visible above the clouds that morning save the roof of Haleakalā, the House of the Sun. Memories flooded my mind as the golden light of morning filled the caldera of this ten-thousand-foot-high volcano (located on the island of Maui). As I thought of my father who was buried thousands of feet below me at Makena Landing, the mountain suddenly disappeared and we were again engulfed in white.

A few moments later I heard a change in the tone of the engines and knew we were beginning our descent toward the Big Island. We continued to be bumped around by the turbid clouds, cloaked in their foreboding opacity. An eerie bluish white light reflected through the windows, reminding me of my ascension in the balloon two and half years before. I tightened my seat belt, uncrossed my legs, and put both feet firmly on the floor. As the plane made a long, steep bank to the right, I felt the landing gear come down and intuitively turned to look out the window.

I couldn't believe what I was seeing. The ground below us was an expanse of bronze- and raven-colored stone. Somehow, I'd again been launched into the cosmos. It looked as if we had taken a wrong turn somewhere and wound up on the *moon!* The only thing that assured me we were not touching down on the lunar surface was the presence of the azure sea.

To my stupefaction, unexpected and undefinable emotions welled up from deep within me as I looked out on wave after wave of black rock. I was totally unashamed when I burst out crying, my tears flowing as copiously as the waterfalls down the cliffs of Kaua'i. The now alarmed flight attendant reached over, touched me, and asked, "Are you okay?"

Barely able to keep myself together, much less maintain any illusion of control, I could only whisper, "I'm home."

Home? Did I say home? She looked at me quizzically, "I thought this was your first trip to the Big Island."

I nodded. "It is."

Never had I felt what I was feeling now. How could I ever explain something so profound that only my heart and soul could possibly understand? Clearly, my brain was out of the loop about whatever was going on here. There was no way I could rationally explain what was going on inside of me, nor was I even tempted to try. I seriously doubted that anyone else would ever be able to understand.

The plane landed and a few moments later made a rolling stop in front of the gate, which was surrounded by clusters of what appeared to be tropical Polynesian huts. *This was an airport?* There were no jetways or high-rise concrete parking lots, only lava rock walls trellised by multicolored bougainvillea and lush tropical vegetation. On the other side of the gate I saw families and friends waving leis, and desperately wished there was someone to welcome me home.

Exiting the plane down an open stairway, I was further overwhelmed by the sensuous smell of the island wafting over me like the finest perfume. I was suffused with a sense of knowing this land and being known by it. There was something exotic and mysterious about this place, yet it felt easy, simple, and real. I felt a sense of serenity that I had never known on this earth. I immediately knew this sacred space held the answers I was searching for. So, too, I was keenly aware that it held many secrets and riddles.

Just before I reached the bottom of the stairs, I swear I heard someone call my name. Without equivocation, I knew the sound I heard was the voice of the land. I stopped instantly when I felt an unseen presence requesting—demanding—that I take off my shoes. I knew I was about to be standing on sacred ground. There, for the first time, the spiritual essence of Hawai'i, the spirit of Aloha, found its way to my soul. The Spiritual Power that I experienced on this *'ainā* (land) was unlike anything I had ever felt before. I knew that nothing less than immediate and wholehearted surrender was required.

Without the slightest hesitation, giving no consideration to what anyone else thought, I removed my shoes, stepped onto the tarmac, got down on my hands and knees, and kissed the ground.

For the first time in my life I knew I was safe. I was home.

A Purple Mountain and Her Majesty, Pele

I quickly found my way to the car rental agency, anxious to see a little of the island in the short time I had. Before receiving my car keys I was required to read rules and regulations about where I could and could not drive on this island and sign an affidavit swearing I would not drive on two roads, South Point Road and Saddle Road. The rules were clear that if I did and had an accident, I was 100 percent liable.

No problem. Unfortunately, I did not have the time to take any scenic tours, as I was scheduled to leave on the first flight the next morning. Besides, I already knew I would be back soon. Before I pulled out, the agent gave me directions to the hotel where my meeting was to take place. It was simple enough—exit the airport and take a left.

I made my way to the two-lane highway that circles the island. However, when I reached the intersection I was flooded with a sense of déjà vu. Something told me to turn right, even though the agent told me to turn left. "Wait a minute . . ." I argued with myself. "I have a meeting in three hours at a resort on the north end of the island and cannot afford to go chasing off based on an intuitive feeling." *Or could I?*

As I sat at the stop sign, the insistent voice echoing from deep inside me was no longer whispering. And the guy behind me also wanted me to make up my mind. Well, something or someone was goading me to make a right turn. Suddenly, my heart vetoed my brain and turned right. I continued driving south until I came to another intersection where the same something-or-other told me, "*Now* turn left."

Okay already.

Well, there I was, moving toward the center of the island. In all honesty, I felt as if the car were driving me, or someone else were driving the car. In any case, there was no doubt in my mind or heart that I was being guided.

Around every corner I crossed an invisible boundary and entered a different world. On one stretch of road it looked as if I were driving across the face of the moon, then I would round a bend where I would be visually overwhelmed by lush tropical flora. It's true what they say about the weather in Hawai'i—that if you don't like it where you are, get in your car and drive ten minutes. Standing on a scenic overlook where the temperature was a dry, hot ninety degrees, I saw a tremendous rainstorm drenching another part of the island. Rainbows filled the air between here and there.

I saw that the land on the Big Island was like a master artist's palette. I was stunned that there could be so many hues and shades of green. The child in me knew the gods and goddesses must have had a grand old time with their color crayons when they created this place.

Several miles up the highway, I found myself in a desert. Gone was the lush vegetation, and in its place were arid golden fields liberally sprinkled with huge cacti and herds of cattle.

As I drove along the winding road, I was constantly covered with goose bumps. I had no idea where I was going, but I was absolutely certain that I was going the right way.

A few minutes later I came up over a small rise and, after making a series of turns, I—or someone—abruptly slammed on the brakes. The tires squealed and left a smoking patch of rubber as the car made a hard, ninety-degree turn to the right. I was shocked and stopped immediately. *What on earth was going on?*

Now, in the past couple years I had gone through more than a few unusual experiences, but this was pushing the limits. Yet, as ludicrous as it may seem, I was now more certain than ever that something with far greater power than I possessed was in control of this trip. I had a deep impression that ignoring my intuition would be the only thing that could get me in trouble.

Thus, I hesitated only slightly when I saw the sign Saddle Road. Well, at this point in the game *nothing* was going to keep me from driving up that mountain. I took a deep breath and said a prayer. I then dropped the car into low gear and headed up the mountain. I figured if I had an accident, I could plead temporary insanity and tell them, "The car made me do it."

I drove up this steep road for several miles, holding my breath more times than I care to recall as huge military vehicles roared past me. It was obvious that this road had been designed by the *Menehune* (Hawaiian leprechauns). As I drove higher up the mountain, voices in my brain nagged at me, telling me that I was now *well* past the elevation that the doctors had told me to stay below. My heart hollered back,

"Ask me if I care!" I was doing what I had to do, rediscovering for the first time since my stay at the treatment center how much I loved breaking the rules.

With every turn of the wheel, my nonrational sense of remembering grew stronger. Of who, or what, or when, I had no idea. All I knew was that if I were going to become a more fully realized human being, I had to continue forward—both in life *and* up this mountain.

Before long I came to the entrance of a large residential development. I stopped in front of the locked electronic gate where the sign said *Waiki'i Ranch.*

A voice deep inside my heart whispered, "This is the place."

"*What* place?" my supposedly rational brain shot back.

No answer.

I parked the car on the side of the road and got out. Ignoring my silk dress, I climbed over the fence. Trespassing? I did not care. I made a beeline—in high heels—across the grassy field, determined to climb to the top of the huge knoll in front of me.

Ten minutes later I huffed and puffed my way over the crest. At that moment the sun broke free from the clouds. I was standing on *my* mountain, and *my* ocean was spread out at my feet. The picture I had been seeing all my life, believing it was only a dream, was real. To my right a brilliant, full rainbow appeared, an iridescent bridge that spanned the heavens, the sea, and the land under my feet. I began to weep with joy, knowing that my tears were releasing toxins left by unremembered sorrows.

I found myself weeping for all the time I had forgotten, for all the years I had been benumbed by others' creeds and deeds. But most of all, I realized I was shedding tears for the part of me that was scared that I would never see home again.

Then I remembered—I had made a commitment to no longer live my life in fear. How could I? Wasn't I even now *living* my dreams? I was *home,* finally delivered to that special place, a place so close to the heart of the earth, a space where my soul felt infinitely safe. This was a sacrosanct place, a womb for my spirit.

On this mountain, under the promise of this dazzling ethereal rainbow, I felt my Goddessential self breathe a sigh of release and relief. As I exhaled, tension poured from my body. As I inhaled the cool mountain air, I realized I was breathing fully and right for the first time in a long time—perhaps ever. I knew that at one time this had indeed been my home. As irrational as it seemed, I actually remembered traveling to a large stone structure that I sensed was several miles to the south, in the shadow of a mountain called Hualālai. I knew this memory came from my soul, that I had been here at another point in another time. Although the impressions were fuzzy, my heart assessment was clear. Standing on the crest of that *puʻu* (hill) I *heard* the spirits of my ancestral family chanting. In silent stillness, my spirit joined them in a hymn of unity. I heard when they called for me to join them on the mountain and immediately answered, "Yes."

I remained on the mountain in a state of grace until it was time to leave for my business meeting. Before the afternoon's agenda was complete, I made a life-changing decision. *I was coming home.*

That afternoon I made a commitment to housesit a home in Waimea (Kamuela), a beautiful community an hour's drive from Kailua-Kona, and I purchased nonrefundable *one-way* tickets for my daughter and myself, and a round-trip ticket for Steve. We were going to return *nine* days later. I did all this without consulting anyone. Steve was already flying to California once a month—I figured he could stay on the plane for lunch. What's more, since the health of our relationship was languishing, an ocean between us did not seem like much more of a barrier than already existed between us.

At the treatment center I had taken a major step in my healing when I decided to abandon all sources of information outside of my inner knowing. I decided to make a wholehearted commitment to listening to, and honoring, my feelings, as well as my personal experiences. A part of me still remembered that the highest purpose of my brain was to be in active and voluntary service to my heart. And my heart wanted to come home. *Now.*

Interestingly enough, my actions met no resistance from Steve. The next day I returned to the mainland and again repacked our belongings. This act of radical trust and total surrender to my intuitive knowing was the genesis of my remembrance.

On August 17, 1990, we returned to Kailua-Kona, where I began an incredible journey across this island of fire.

Deep Waters

Within a few minutes of landing in Kailua-Kona we had an auspicious meeting with a local realtor and an hour later signed a lease on a beautiful home. From our lanai with a panoramic view of the entire Kona coast, it seemed obvious that we were supposed to be here. Before Steve returned to the mainland a week later, he began to make queries about joining or setting up a practice on the Big Island or commuting to O'ahu.

At least once a week I drove to Waiki'i Ranch, feeling drawn toward that magic space. Over the next months I met both the owner and sales manager of the development. Sensing the depth of my spiritual connection with this land, they gave me the security code to the gate, telling me I was welcome on the property any time.

The owner told me that a number of years before, he had mortgaged everything he owned to buy this stunning property. He'd done so in spite of the fact that he'd been told that there was no water to support the development. But he knew in his heart that this was not the case. He could *feel* the water. Following his gut, he continued to ignore the supposed geological experts who advised him that he was pouring money down dry holes. Drilling deeper and deeper beneath the rich topsoil of Waiki'i, they one day hit water. They tapped into deep wells that were continually replenished with what would be an unlimited supply of fresh water. Granted, it would take jet engines to bring the water thousands of feet to the surface, but his knowing was true. The water *was* there.

I never journeyed to or across Saddle Road without stopping to make an offering of respect to Pele, the goddess of fire. Soon after I moved to the islands, a friend and I built an altar in a large field of ʻaʻā lava (rough, broken lava), with views of the peaks of Mauna Keʻa, Mauna Loa, Hualālai, and Haleakalā, on the island of Maui. For me this was a personal sacred site. I, like the Hawaiians, believe that ancestral spirits reside within these stones.

Countless people I know, both locals and visitors, have experienced what they believe to be direct physical encounters with Pele while traveling this road and others. Some encounter her as an old and wise crone, while others are met by a beautiful young woman. Almost always she is accompanied by a small white dog.

I, too, would almost daily encounter spirits. However, some of my visits were from psychological shadows, pieces from my recent past. Soon, much of what I'd thought of as normal or otherwise real was laid to rest. More than once my brain and heart came to loggerheads over something that I'd previously been indoctrinated to believe was supernatural. But truth prevailed as it always will, and I discovered that what we often call miracles are quite ordinary. I began to discover that faith is in many ways antithetical to my previous religious beliefs. My brain was now redeemed, and in many ways it was my fledgling but unflinching belief in reincarnation that became the cornerstone that supported my new life. What others might deny or ascribe to happenstance was the universe unfolding in divine order. I realized that I was a spiritual being, here on Earth to experience the wonders of being in a physical body, having emotional and intellectual experiences. Suddenly, life seemed so simple. Miracles became ordinary events. What I had before interpreted as random anomalies began to take on a definite pattern.

Time: And Time Again

Shortly after arriving on the island, I woke up unusually early one morning and intuitively knew I was *supposed* to go around the island to Volcanoes National Park. This would be my first of many sojourns to Halemaʻumaʻu crater.

When I arrived, I made the short walk to the edge of the caldera, where I made the traditional offering of gin and a lei. Even though the crater was dry, with only wisps of steam escaping fissures in the crust, I felt intimidated. I sensed my utter insignificance as the raw energy of Gaia percolated under my feet. As I meditated in the vaporous presence of this natural power, I became aware as never before that if we do not love and heal this planet, Goddessence help us, she will heal herself. And probably when we least expect it.

During my long moments of contemplation, I was unaware that I was being observed. As I prepared to leave, a park ranger approached me. Following a genial conversation, he asked if I'd like to join him and his partner, a woman, on a hike to check the south flank, where a vent was currently flowing. I was dumbfounded. "Are you kidding?" They were not.

Several hours later we were standing on a piece of the newest land on the planet, ground that had been birthed only weeks before. The air temperature was well over one hundred degrees, and the earth was so hot that I had genuine concern for the soles of my shoes. In retrospect, I might have been a bit more concerned for my overall physical safety.

The rangers left me alone as I sat spellbound, gazing into the bowels of the earth, looking through a two-by-three-foot hole in Gaia's fragile crust, a geological opening known as a *skylight*. There, only inches away, molten lava more than two thousand degrees Fahrenheit flowed like water, coursing its way to the sea. The sheer force of fiery energy being discharged from the core of the planet was hypnotic. My rational brain was absolutely oblivious to danger as this river of fire flowed only inches beneath my feet.

Several miles away Pele was claiming what She would, engulfing virtually all homes in a subdivision known as Kalapana Gardens. At that moment she was sitting down to devour Kalapana's famous black sand beach and its halo of majestic, verdant palms. She would also claim as her own the ancient Queen's Bath and purify by fire a number of ancient *heiaus* (temples).

What happened next stunned me to a new level. As I sat there, utterly mesmerized, I heard a woman—not an inner voice, but an external voice—say to me, "I want your time."

What?

The disembodied voice became more adamant, "I *want* your time."

"I *heard* you," I fired back. "I'm just not sure I get what you mean."

Intuitively, I then looked down at the expensive gold watch on my wrist. NO. It had been a gift. *Surely,* She *couldn't* want my watch.

She repeated, "I want your time."

By now I knew that arguing with this voice was futile. I knew it would be the same as someone on a tricycle squabbling with a disgruntled private sitting behind the wheel of a military supply truck for the right of way on Saddle Road. Not me. All too clearly I realized that if she wanted my life, she could take it as easily as she was consuming homes in Kalapana.

Without further ado, I took off my watch, blessed it and the giver, and thanked it for serving me well. Whispering a prayer, I dropped it into the skylight without a single regret.

My conceptions, judgments, and sentiments about time—the illusion of a past, present, and future—were the offerings life was requiring of me. No doubt about it, many of my issues of control and illusion were wrapped up in the hands of my watch. That day, both Pele and the island put me on notice that unconditional surrender was the lesson I was here to learn. Immediately, I became a willing pupil.

Intersections in Time and Space: Turning Points

Without looking for them, I began to have intuitive, psychic experiences. These were to affect my life in significant ways. Nothing in my background had equipped me to deal with *any* of these phenomena. More than once I challenged whatever Higher Power was listening: "Hey! Enough already! All I asked for was a safe place. I wasn't looking for these otherworldly encounters. Dying was quite enough, thank you. Can we turn off the tap, please?"

The answer was a resounding *"No."* I realized that I'd made a commitment and put my foot to the path and there was to be no turning back.

At first, I studiously avoided anything "New Age." Mind you, this is *not* an easy thing to do in Hawai'i. I steered clear of anyone with a flowing white robe or a name like El Abbadabbado, Twinkle, Aurora, Star, or Swami Beyondashadowofadoubt.

But increasingly, I met people who were "channeling" esoteric entities from who-knows-where, Buddhist lamas, and others who talked regularly with E.T.s and angels. Then there were the people who considered themselves "walk-ins," who believed that the bodies they were in were not their own, but that they were actually migrating souls who had taken over other people's bodies for some higher purpose. Okayyyyyy . . . . . Well, mind you, some of these folks had some pretty interesting stuff to say. As hard as it sometimes was, I attempted to remain open to whatever wisdom resonated with or reflected my own inner knowing. I knew (know) and loved (still love 'em) people who were literally building landing pads in the middle of remote lava fields for inbound UFOs.

Amazingly, though, many of these metaphysically far-out people were running significant, successful, and *normal* businesses.

In my first few months on the island I grew in my capacity to love and came to honor and respect all paths. Many of these people became close acquaintances; a few became dear friends. All the same, I determined that dying had been enough of a "way-out" experience for me.

All I cared about at this point was not accelerating what was already going on in my life.

You see, I was discovering that sliding back into my body was a lot easier than staying put. I wanted more than anything to remember what I had seen and learn how to get my feet firmly planted back on the earth. During this time I intentionally did not read spiritual books, participate in metaphysical/spiritual workshops, or visit psychics. I defined my spiritual path primarily as one of being open to my dreams. It had become my habit in the past couple years to write or paint whatever or whomever showed up in these nocturnal excursions.

From November of 1990 through February of 1991 I would go through a progressive series of spiritual experiences and encounters connected to one word—*Remember.* The initial event happened in the middle of the night while on a trip to Florida.

I had awakened from a dream where again I saw myself as a child. I remembered hearing someone in my dream tell me that I was only a reflection. Somehow this seemed to dovetail with my growing obsession about the Pattern and holography. I knew there was far more to this dream than what little I could bring to consciousness.

I kept a journal in which I daily wrote down my dreams and processed any lingering thoughts. The following is an excerpt of the entry I made in my journal the morning of November 11, 1990:

The Potpourri of Me — Integration

NOVEMBER 11, 1990

Childhood. Those were days where I struggled to figure out who I was, what I wanted, and how on earth I fit in amidst the clanging cymbals of

clashing cultures . . . all the while twisting on a torture rack called perfec-
tion . . .

    Am I a reflection? Yes.

    But today the pond is muddy, stirred by swirling surface winds. The
heavens are covered by clouds of elephant gray whose shadows obscure the
surface, hiding the monsters who lurk below this watery opaque grave . . .

    How can a reflection see itself? How can it know of itself what it is of?
Through the clouds and tears there is a glimmer of Light.

    It takes another . . . a reflection is seen only in the Light . . .

    Yet, a reflection is absolute, full, known in nature . . . seen only when
there is Light . . . seen only when another is willing to look . . . seen differ-
ently by others . . . seen from their position and perspective . . .

    A reflection is clear, bright, fragrant, translucent, iridescent Light. It is
Love that allows peace to ride on the rainbow of truth that bridges the
universe—Love is all that is carried by all who indeed, and in deed, stand
in the Light.

    Looking at these words I knew there was a clue here about the Pat-
tern. I wanted to paint a rainbow but somehow knew the Pattern was
not a normal rainbow.

    This was followed by a second experience later the same day.

    On this day I was driving south on the Florida turnpike to visit my
son.

    Out of the blue I heard a very powerful woman's voice.

    "There's no room for me to join you in this car," she said.

    Oh, great. Here we go again, I thought. But immediately, I turned
off my radar detector and slowed down to the speed limit. Glancing
around the rental car I had been driving for two weeks, I had to acknowledge that she—whoever she was—was right. The car looked like
a cross between a closet and a dumpster. By now, I knew better than to
ignore my Voices.

    I cruised in to the next service center and began to clean the car. I even went so far as to borrow a hand-held vacuum cleaner from a truck driver. I then proceeded to wash the car, using the high-powered hose meant for blasting mashed bugs off the grills of semis.

Once the car was spick-and-span, I climbed back in, fully expecting the Voice to acknowledge my efforts. Silence. "Thanks a lot," I said to the void as I sat—obviously alone—in my now thoroughly disinfected car. "Now I'm going to be thirty minutes late for my appointment. All for nothing."

It was after two in the morning by the time I finished the last of the day's activities in Ft. Lauderdale. An unexpected evening meeting had run longer than I anticipated. Once again, I had been through a series of *chance* encounters, each providing another piece of the enigmatic puzzle that had become my life.

When I finally left, it was pouring rain. I said my good-byes and made a dash for my car. I got in, and without a thought, threw an armful of soggy papers I'd collected onto the front passenger seat.

I was about to start the engine when, out of the nothingness, came the Voice.

"Where am I to sit?" she asked innocently.

Holding my breath, I grabbed all the things that I had just tossed onto the seat and was out of the car in a flash. As I stood in the downpour, my curiosity momentarily abandoned me. I was no longer certain that I wanted to get back in the car. My friends who were watching me leave called out, "Is everything okay?"

"Sure. Everything is fine," I reassured them. I couldn't help but recall my favorite acronym for fear—Forget Everything And Run! Where were my *supersonic get-me-outta-here sneakers* when I really needed them? I walked to the back of the car, opened the trunk, and dumped my papers inside. I then muttered a prayer, returned to the driver's door, and got in.

I took a deep breath and prepared to dive into the cosmic ethers. "Okay. Here's the deal, ma'am. I have a long drive ahead of me, but you're more than welcome to come along for the ride."

God, was I really talking to an empty seat?

Carefully backing out of the driveway, I nonchalantly reached over and turned on the radio, thinking the music would help keep me awake. Fifty yards down the road, as I pulled up to a stop sign, the Voice softly but emphatically challenged me. "Are you going to turn off the radio or am I?"

Awareness flashed through my being at the speed of light. Immediately the palm of my hand flew up and I hit the off button on the radio. The Voice was hard enough to handle; I did not need or want any physical demonstrations. Shaking with cold and fear, I opened my mouth for the last time that night and surrendered. "Okay. I give up. Just get me to North Palm Beach safely."

The tone of this Voice was only of love, so I knew it must be that of a guide or a teacher sent for my education and edification.

The next thing I remember was taking the key out of the ignition in front of my friend's home. The two-hour drive was, and remains, a total blank except for the single phrase that echoed though my entire being—"Look for the *Pattern*."

I knew I was finally getting close to remembering!

CHAPTER EIGHT

Tapestry: Weft and Warp

Cataracts of the Heart

*B*y December 1990, war was threatening in the Persian Gulf. Although I felt relatively safe in Hawai'i, I also felt a paradoxical sense of pending doom mixed with my hope for illumination and remembrance.

The gloom I felt had nothing to do with events in the Middle East; it was for my relationship with Steve. I felt blinded by dense cataracts of the heart, occlusions that kept me from seeing many things, including, I suspected, the Pattern.

Though I was usually glad to see him arrive, I was becoming equally disturbed by the sense of relief I felt when he left. I couldn't help but note that this was living proof of another emotional mistruth—that absence does not make the heart grow fonder. Now that we were thousands of miles apart, I experienced a growing awareness of how separate we really were. The space between us was not the sacred space Kahlil Gibran speaks of; it was a seemingly unbridgeable rift that our disparate experiences had cleaved between our hearts. It was a distance far greater than time zones could measure, and neither of us could get from "here" to "there" via an airplane ride.

By our first anniversary things were rapidly deteriorating. Even though the time between Steve's visits now often stretched to four or five weeks, we both refused to give up on our marriage. This, despite that fact I saw little in the way of tangible evidence that he would ever relocate to Hawai'i. My truth was that he was making little effort to sever the chains that bound him to the Midwest.

Sadly, in spite of the hundreds of hours of individual therapy that we had each gone through, we were not able to make it work for *us*. In January of 1991, we made an attempt at coming together by attending a relationship intensive workshop in the Washington, D.C., area. I hoped that this workshop would mark a turning point in our marriage. It did, but not the one I anticipated.

While there, it became obvious that we were stymied in our attempts to understand the dynamic happening between us. I felt compassion for what Steve had gone through relative to my profound changes following the accident. This was because I, too, was now realizing that I missed the man I'd eventually married—not the one I met three years before, but the man who, after his stay at the treatment center, was for a short while not hyper, frenzied, or rabidly intense. I missed the man who was, for a while, calm, balanced, and easygoing.

We were simply two very different people. We had changed costumes, but we were still simultaneously playing all the parts in a never-ending game of relational charades. Only now neither the pain nor the game was covert.

I had traveled more than five thousand miles for a two-day workshop. I believed then and believe now with all my heart that relationship is humankind's unique opportunity to work out all our spiritual stuff—our own salvation, if you will. I looked at our marriage vows— "for better or worse"—and knew that if we didn't make changes now, it was going to get much worse before it would ever get better. I knew that our marriage was affording us the opportunity to heal many of our deepest wounds, but I also knew we could not take much more wounding.

As we sat in that workshop on that cold January day, I could not help but again wonder if perhaps this was the Pattern. Doubt was beating me black and blue as the word *pattern* ricocheted off the canyon walls of my brain. Might it merely be a repressed wound reminding me to look at my life situation from a different perspective?

No. There was more to it. In both my gut and heart I knew that this Pattern was somehow love, but that there was much more to this love than sentiment or some gooey feeling. I was more determined than ever that I would not have to die again in order to remember it.

As the weekend passed, I felt I had failed. I could not get Steve to hear that my feelings had little, if anything, to do with him. I could not seem to get through to him that I did not want him to be the "doctor" in our relationship. I did not want or need him to fix me. I just wanted him to hear me. I wanted him to hold me until I didn't hurt anymore. All I wanted was for the anger to stop.

I needed him to know that "the other woman" could not come back. I tried to help him understand that in many ways I was grateful for the accident, and that my "death" and subsequent change were not anyone's fault. Although I was able to acknowledge and thank him for bringing me back twice, neither of us could get past our fears.

Looking back, I think we both knew that change was imminent, the signs of pending emotional disaster written on the wall. The only question was how much longer we could stay in our old characters and keep playing the roles. We'd been together long enough to know the script by heart. We had committed every line to memory. I was sad, sorry in many ways, but knew if we couldn't find a new script it would soon be time to close the show.

Assault on the Soul: Hostilities against the Heart

Following the workshop I remained in Washington. Our capital was now the center of global attention as America threatened to open a hellacious conflict in the Persian Gulf.

Were knuckling under to the harassment of a bully and bullying back with bigger sticks and bigger stones the only answers? Why is it that the vast majority of the wars waged on this planet are fought in God's name? Isn't God about love? Could we afford to again try to justify a war by egonomics and economics? Were we as a nation going to be permanently stuck in greedlock? I was terrified, sensing that we were about to descend into depravity, attempting once more to bring about peace by waging war.

On January 16, I was landing at Washington's National Airport (returning from a one-day business trip to New York) when the pilot announced that America was at war. The tempest known as Operation Desert Storm had just begun. Exiting the plane, a group of six passengers, all of us total strangers, spontaneously found ourselves locked in a tearful group embrace. Like little children, we were scared, and without hesitation sought consolation from one another. We were like-minded travelers who intuitively knew that this deranged war would not be the catalyst to a new world order.

Like all other wars, Operation Desert Storm left overt and covert wounds that for many would refuse to heal. I felt that I had prayed in vain. I saw all too clearly that my own relationship was a microcosm of the global macrocosm. I saw that my most painful injuries came when I was caught in the crossfire of judgment and blame.

All I could do was continue to pray that one day we would all awaken to the Goddessence of ourselves and have the courage and conviction to stand for a new paradigm of peace. I could only hope that one day we would honor what was honest, pure, good, and just.

How long would it take for humankind to see *this* pattern—the pattern of hate—and learn that there could be no accord through armed contest? Why couldn't we once and for all get it in our brains and hearts that God is not somewhere out there? God is not watching us from a distance! How long would it take for us to realize that the Divine is inherent within each and every one of us? How long would we as a global human community—a family—continue to *act* out rather than *work* out our aggression? How long would it take before we saw that any hostile act of aggression would only inflict ruin upon the spirits of all nations?

My heart broke, for I believed we were betraying the children—the children who are all of us. Again we were sacrificing the souls of the men and women—fathers and mothers, brothers and sisters—who were sucked into the quagmire of this psychotic charade.

It was during this time that I made a life-changing decision, breaking old and heavy shackles of fear. Glued to CNN as scuds fell on Israel, I held hands with my terrified friends as they attempted to reach family living there. I will never forget the moment I realized my soul was ready to embrace my purpose and be a catalyst for love. There, in that moment, I resolved to be more than a conscientious objector—I determined that peace was to be my soul's conscious objective.

The Pattern of Healing!
Dreamscapes and Dreamshapes

For most of my adult life, Valentine's Day ranked as my most detested holiday.

Not since adolescence had Cupid ranked with Santa Claus or the Tooth Fairy. Many years ago I figured out that this annual celebration of romance only reinforces illusions of white picket fences, knights in shining armor, and happily-ever-afters. Yes, as a child, I'd adorned the requisite shoe box, decorating it with paper doilies, red ribbons, and hearts. Valentine's Day was one of the most highly anticipated party days in elementary school. It was a prepubescent date with fantasy, the one day a year we could exchange without embarrassment our juvenile tokens of love. Like many others, I spent days writing proclamations of budding love or abiding friendship. At the same time, I was filled with utter agony, terrified that when I opened my whimsical mailbox it would be empty.

Well, my dread of the empty box came true again. Steve was due to arrive in Kailua-Kona at noon on Valentine's Day, and our plan was to go to a resort for dinner and an evening of dancing. However, the night before, he called to tell me he was not going to make it home until the nineteenth due to a change in his surgery schedule. Once again, the day intended for showing and sharing love became a wake. In my loneliness I never imagined that on this night I would remember the Pattern and experience more of love than I ever dreamed of embracing in this lifetime.

At 3:00 A.M. on Valentine's Day 1991, I sat bolt upright in bed, covered with "chicken skin"—Hawaiian goose bumps. It was as if the hurricane-force winds blowing in my dream had propelled me back into this world. I had seen the Pattern! The vision I saw in my dream was exceedingly clear, vivid, and absolutely real. The Pattern was not an illusion! It was not a figment of my imagination.

Through my dream state, I had again made a sojourn into another realm, a dimension that usually remains invisible unless a divine light illuminates its presence. Just because we cannot see something does not mean it is not there!

In my dream, I moved toward the Light, heading for the end of what I knew was the same tunnel I had voyaged through four years before. Only this time, the woman who'd been in my car three months ago was guiding me. Leading me gently by the hand, she assured me that I had nothing to fear, and I knew that I was not going to die. In any case, I wasn't afraid of death because I knew the truth. Death isn't real, and it most certainly isn't the end. Giving up the physical body is only a transition that we as spiritual beings make to go on to our next genesis. If death is the end, then why do I and so many others remember being dead?

Hand in hand, my guide and I ventured to the end of the tunnel, where we looked out into the universe. It was there, standing on the precipice of eternity, that I saw the fields of time and space merge. There, poised on the edge of infinity, I again saw the Pattern—a matrix that was somehow singular, yet as vast as the stars.

I managed to find my voice and ask, "What is it?"

The Voice belonging to the hand that firmly held mine replied, "It is the Pattern of Healing."

This time I knew I would remember.

I have no memory of turning around or moving backward, yet I was suddenly sitting upright in my bed, as wide awake as I have ever been.

Reweaving the Strands of Light and Love: The Heart of Intimacy

I got out of bed and raced downstairs to my office, knowing that I had to find a pencil and paper. I had to capture the Pattern as best I could—a considerable challenge, because I had abandoned my art career in kindergarten, after mastering stick figures, rainbows, and happy faces.

Six hours, one full eraser, and a sixty-four-count box of color crayons later, I finally had it. Well, let's say, a version of it.

My original drawings looked something like this:

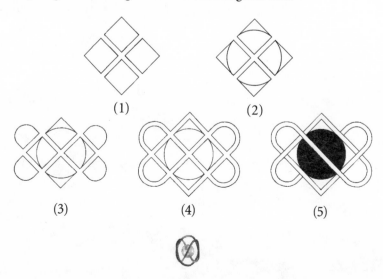

(1)   (2)

(3)   (4)   (5)

The first thing I drew was (1) empty space, a window of the four diamonds floating in the void. This void then birthed (2) the Sphere, the feminine, passive polestar of the evolving Pattern. Next came (3) four vacuous crescents, a quad of crowns wreathing the single circle that served to take that which was still explicit in its formlessness to yet a fuller state of emptiness. Then (4), when an unbroken single line encompassed all the pieces, the vacuum was filled, the context defined, yet the connection incomplete. Only when the rainbowlike strands of light and love were correctly woven did (5) the fragments meld, and the whole—the Pattern—emerge. There were eight hearts, four squares, one circle, the numbers three and eight, and upright and inverted pyramids.

I was astounded. All the shapes I had been seeing for so long really were the same. All were pieces of a single whole. Little did I know (thank goodness) that before much longer I would begin a very long series of initiations. Over time the universe would ask me to surrender all my old ideas, as well as virtually all my material possessions. I would have to come to a place where I realized that enlightenment comes only when we are standing in the lightness of the nothingness. Years later I would remember that it was the teacher named Jesus who said, "My yoke is easy, my burden is light." He carried love, which isn't weighty. It isn't a burden. It is Light—infinite, luminous, and clear Light.

To say that this remembrance was an emotional epiphany would be an understatement. After a four-year pursuit of my personal grail, finding the Pattern marked a turning point in the development of my essential spiritual awareness. The whole process had induced a state of mindfulness, and on Valentine's Day 1991, I began what I knew would be nothing less than a lifelong quest into Love.

I suspected the first thing to do was to begin to figure out what the Pattern meant to me. Very quickly it became the compass for my life, an inner guidance system of sorts that I would use to set and then correct my course.

One of the very first things I did was fax a copy of my drawing to Lael. Within hours we were bouncing off the satellites between southern California and Hawai'i.

Deciding to start with the basics, I got out the dictionary to look up the word *heal*. I found synonyms and related words like *restoration, grace, rejuvenation, peace, amnesty, absolution, reconciliation, armistice, reparation, truce, harmony, renovation, resuscitation, reclamation, forgive, pacify, remedy,* and *revive*. Each word motivated me to look deeper into those areas in my life that still needed to be healed. Soon Spirit peeled back the layers and revealed a few gaping wounds that I had earlier plastered with psychic Band-Aids.

I also did not have to look far to see that the entire world was suffering from a multitude of ailments that the global human family needed to address and heal. As I watched television, listened to the radio, and read the newspaper, I saw that every system of creation was frail and suffering.

The Pattern was my final call to wake up to the fact that we are spiritual beings here on Earth. I knew from that day forward that I would no longer be allowed to walk or talk in my sleep.

I began to pray as never before, asking the Life Force of the universe for wisdom and understanding. I desired to know what the Pattern truly was, as well as to integrate its essential truth into all the areas of my life. I knew this was nonnegotiable if I were to fulfill my purpose. Having been told by the *presence* four years before that I was to be a catalyst for change, for love, I knew that the Pattern was the heart of my purpose—for only one word defined what it so graphically illustrated—Love, wholehearted, unconditional Love.

Embers from Our Island Home

The most important task at hand centered on my relationship with Steve. I was committed to working it out, but not if it killed me. The

Gulf War was undermining Hawai'i's economy; consequently, Steve's dream—which I had been putting all of my time and energy into—was dissolving. Even though our relationship was eroding almost as quickly, I continued to fill one emotional sandbag after another, hoping to keep the flood of tears at bay as long as possible.

On April 17, 1991, we went to the Polynesian Cultural Center on O'ahu to see an IMAX film entitled *The Polynesian Odyssey*. This large-screen film is a masterpiece that graphically chronicles the sea voyage made by the earliest inhabitants of the Hawaiian islands. It is stunning in its realistic portrayal of these courageous people's journey.

At the close of the film, music began to play that riveted me to my seat. I began to cry, and when the screen went black, I cried on. And on. And on. Soon the theater was empty, but I could not move and my tears felt endless. Steve sat next to me, and all I could say was, "The music. The music."

Finally, a big Hawaiian *bruddah* who was manning the door came over to us and said, "Folks, I'm sorry, but I have to ask you to leave. It's time for the next show."

Reluctantly, I got up from my seat and we exited the theater. I was upset because I could not remember the words to the song, save one phrase, "Embers from our island home." Interestingly, that was all Steve could recall as well.

Imagination or Magic?

Two and a half months later my children and I were in Honolulu for an overnight excursion. The express purpose for me was to take them to see the film so I could hear the music again. I wanted to write down the words, and I also had a feeling that somehow hearing this music would help my children understand why I had to be in Hawai'i. As they saw it, Mom was stuck on this shoal, stalled in the middle of the Pacific Ocean.

As the three of us sat in the theater, engrossed in the epic tale, Julia kept turning to me and asking, "So, when's the music coming on?"

"In a minute. In a minute," I replied, "it's at the end."

Suddenly the credits were rolling, the screen went black, and the same Hawaiian young man was announcing, "Thank you for sharing our adventure. Please exit through the doorways to your right."

I was dumbfounded, and the kids were looking at me more than slightly askance. "Soooooo, Mommmmm . . ." they echoed in unison. Julia finished their shared thought, "So, what about the music? I didn't hear any music. How 'bout you, Ryan?"

I was livid! I could not figure out why they would edit the song out of the film. Further, it seemed to me the film lacked the aliveness that it had the first time I saw it.

With the kids in tow, I headed left instead of right, planting myself in front of the guy behind the microphone. "Why on earth did you edit the music out of the film?" I demanded.

He looked at me curiously and responded, "What music?"

Wrong answer. "Oh no. No. No. No. I was here on April 17 and there was music. It played for the last few minutes of the film and through the credits. It was wonderful. It was magical."

Julia and Ryan were becoming embarrassed, taking on the posture of parentally induced mortification as only kids can. The young man sensed I was not through.

"Listen, the music is the only reason I drove out here today. I wanted my children to hear the music." I was near tears.

Then this man was suddenly looking at me differently. "I remember you. I couldn't figure out what was wrong with you that day."

"Nothing was wrong," I replied. "Everything was right. It was the music."

"Ma'am, I don't know what to say except to tell you that I was on the production crew for this film, and there never was any music." He saw the look on my face and held up his hand, "Listen. I don't doubt at all that you heard music, but the music must have been just for you."

I was stunned, and I'm sure my kids thought, "Oh, no. Here we go again . . . "

I immediately thanked him and hightailed it to a pay phone, where I called Steve on the mainland. Once he was on the line, I asked, "Please tell me what happened the day we were at the Polynesian Cultural Center."

"What do you mean?" he queried.

"No, Steve, I'm not going to play Twenty Questions. Just tell me what happened," I replied.

"Are you talking about the music?" he asked.

"Right. Tell me about the music."

He simply and clearly recounted the experience. I wasn't losing my mind.

"Well, funny thing, Steve. The kids and I just saw the film and there wasn't any music. As a matter of fact the guy at the door says there never was any music. So, what do you think of that?"

He did not know what to think. Neither did I. Part of me was sick, thinking how for four years I struggled to remember the Pattern before I finally retrieved it. Now this music, the song. How could I hear something so beautiful that was never there in the first place?

Or was it?

Hypnosis or Hype?

A couple weeks later I was at a party on the beach in Kailua-Kona visiting with a friend, Dr. Leonard Laskow. Lenny is an M.D., a healer from the San Francisco area. As we sat talking on the beach, I shared the experience with him. Fascinated, he immediately suggested that I undergo hypnosis to see if the song could be retrieved. I thought this was a great idea and asked who I should go to.

"Lynnclaire, there's only one person I would trust to put you under," he responded.

I took the bait. "Who's that?"

"Dr. Irv Katz," he replied.

"Okay. So where do I have to go to find this guy?"

Lenny laughed as he replied, "He's the one sitting on the red ice chest." He pointed to the friendly face near the picnic tables.

Irv was a psychologist residing on the island of Maui. He has an extensive background in hypnosis and is committed to empowering others to delve into their life purposes as well as their personal psychospiritual work. After I repeated the story to him, Irv agreed to do the session and we set up an appointment to work together the following Monday.

Monday afternoon arrived and Irv, Lenny, and I met at Irv's hotel. Soon we were set up and ready to go, recording the session so that we would have the words to the song if I recalled them.

Irv counted me down, and before long I was telling him the precise location of the theater seats; I was even able to recall clearly what other tourists around me were wearing.

"So, Lynnclaire, tell me about the music that you and Steve heard," Irv said.

I replied, "Steve did not hear the music. He heard an echo."

Then the tape recorder stopped. Both Irv and Lenny attempted to get it working again, but to no avail. Finally Irv continued the session without it. As he probed, they learned that I had indeed heard the music. What's more, I knew all the words. But when I shared the lyrics with them, no one had the time to write them down.

Unfortunately, I was watching the whole thing but could not hear anything. As nonrational as it was, at some point in the regression I left my body and sat high in the corner of the room looking down on the scene. I saw my mouth moving on what I knew was my body, but I was deaf. I was not afraid, although I do recall being surprised, wondering what I was doing "up there" again. I watched as Irv and Lenny appeared to be in a fairly intense conversation with me.

Then, in another instant, I was back in my body.

Wouldn't you know, as soon as Irv began to walk me back into consciousness, the tape recorder began recording.

After what seemed like a fifteen-minute session at most, I opened my eyes. When fully awake I was informed that almost two hours had passed.

"Did the words come back or not?" I asked.

"Oh, yes. More than the words to the song came back. But you weren't there, were you?" Irv asked.

I shook my head, perplexed.

"Do you remember where you were?" Irv asked.

"I was up there," I responded, pointing to the ceiling. "Did anyone write them down?"

Lenny answered, "Unfortunately, no."

I was disappointed, but was even then learning to release my attachment to outcome and expectations. At least I knew the words were real.

At 3:00 A.M. that morning, for the second time in six months, I sat bolt upright in bed. I heard every word of the song playing in my head and flew to my computer to write them down. Then, at this ungodly hour, I picked up the phone and called Irv.

"No problem," he said, as I began to apologize, "I'm the one who told you to do it!"

It seemed that Irv had left a posthypnotic suggestion that I would call him after I had awakened and written down the words.

Does the song have anything to do with the Pattern?

You decide.

Embers of Starfire

As teachers and healers we've been called by Hawai'i,
Our light giving life to the shared vision we see,
For we know we're the strands of an ancient heirloom tapestry,
Woven, designed, and preserved in the Light of Eternity.
For we are remnants of fire guided to a safe place,
Our being fully known in this sacred space,
Called here together, family drawn from afar,
Shielding a spark of memory, embers from our island home
upon a distant star.

Threads all unique, smooth, rich, subtle, some bright,
Yet woven together we reflect only the Light.
Liquid silver the fabric, stardust blown on the breeze,
Spirits here blanket the earth and now heal with ease.
For we are remnants of fire guided to a safe place,
Our being fully known in this sacred space,
Called here together, family drawn from afar,
Shielding a spark of memory, embers from our island home
upon a distant star.

Memories locked in the shadow, obscured for so long,
From darkness released, keys turn in dream and song.
Gliding a ribbon of stars we pressed toward the dawn,
Grasping a sliver of knowing, our light burning strong.
For we are remnants of fire guided to a safe place,
Our being fully known in this sacred space,
Called here together, family drawn from afar,
Shielding a spark of memory, embers from our island home
upon a distant star.

Called home for reunion, each remembered once more,
Our shared vision recalled, the brilliant flame now restored.
Ascend from these islands, empowered by this sacred space,
Lifting a torch of remembrance, to light the world with grace.
For we are remnants of fire guided to a safe place,
Our being fully known in this sacred space,
Called here together, family drawn from afar,
Shielding a spark of memory, embers from our island home
upon a distant star.

Stars and Starry Eyed: Or Stark, Raving Mad?

Six weeks later Steve and I were again trying to cool the flames in our stalemated relationship, as well as evade the summer heat, when we took our bed outside to sleep on the lanai. With the Milky Way glistening over our heads, I tried to explain to him what it was like to stand at the end of the tunnel. We were talking about the Pattern and the song "Embers of Starfire" when suddenly the light all around us began to change. Then, there in the ebony sky, we both saw the Pattern. It was a huge display of light that illuminated the heavens, lasting only a minute or two at the most. Then, stunning both of us, time and space seemed to warp back to "normal." Two nights later the same thing happened while my friend, a Jungian analyst from Israel, and I were sitting on the front lawn. Again, I sat spellbound.

I have been and remain extremely grateful for the witnesses who have been beside me on every step of this journey. Nonetheless, my mother has suggested I call this a book of fiction, insisting that no one would ever believe it was the truth.

Yet, who could ever make up such a saga?

CHAPTER NINE

The Life Force of Eight

Mystical Paths

*H*awaiʻi is in many ways uniquely out of sync with linear time. These islands seem to move to a different rhythm. Here the sun, moon, stars, the gods and goddesses, chimeras of yesteryear and beyond, walk profoundly in the present. For many, the spirits of their ancestors are close to the surface of their awareness. So, too, my soul was becoming more and more attuned to the reality of these worlds than to the "real" world an ocean away.

Time continued to erode, etching new lines in my heart, as day after day I lived with the Pattern. Though I was still uncertain what I was meant to do with it, the Pattern nonetheless continued to evoke a remembrance of a Love that was primordial. In many ways it served to keep me connected to my soul.

Others I shared it with seemed moved and also saw this simple form as a symbol of Love. In spite of my personal, crumbling experience within an intimate relationship, I knew at the core of my being that the

Love the Pattern reflected was attainable and w-holy sustainable. Yet there was so much I didn't understand.

One night, friends invited me to dinner to meet a Hawaiian *kahuna*, one of the keepers of Hawai'i's spiritual path, *Huna*. Kahunas are spiritual teachers, those who have been trained in the ways of their ancestors. Although I had met many who considered themselves kahunas, I knew that most respected teachers were trained in the language of silence. Ask a Hawaiian for an introduction to a kahuna, and your request will often be met with silence. For generations they were prohibited from speaking openly of the esoteric, ancestral mysteries. The history of the Hawaiian people, like that of so many other indigenous peoples, taught them that to do so would result in the degradation of the sovereign spirit of aloha. Huna had never been abandoned; it had merely gone underground for divine protection. True kahunas only share knowledge when they are guided. Although the mystical truths of Huna are gradually being revealed, you will never find a true kahuna in the yellow pages.

My friends put me on notice that this fellow was an eccentric character. But they thought that if he met me, he might be able and, more important, be willing to talk with me about the Pattern.

This man was definitely an original, and I liked him immediately. However, for some reason he was not willing to talk about the Pattern in front of a group. He suggested that we excuse ourselves, and we went outside. Sitting in the carport (because it was raining), I watched in silence as he contemplated my drawing. After a long moment he raised his head, looked me straight in the eye, and said, "I will allow you to ask one question and I will answer this one question fully to the best of my ability."

Only one question? Didn't he know I had a million?

I thought for a long while before responding and could hardly believe the words I heard exit my mouth. "What is the significance of the number eight?"

I was furious at myself. "Who on earth is chairwoman of the board in my brain tonight?" I wondered, berating myself. This was indeed one of my many questions, as the number eight is represented sixteen times in the Pattern. But this hardly seemed the most important of the Pattern's mysteries.

But he looked at me with a knowing smile, and I sensed that I had asked the appropriate question.

He replied, "The answers you seek come from the stars. All the answers are within you.

"There is a name that has been passed down through my family for generations. My auntie now carries the name that is also your name and the name of this pattern. The key is the number eight."

He continued. "You see, the Hawaiian people believe—no, we know—that we have descended from the stars. We believe this quite literally. Our ancestors came to Earth from a constellation known as the Pleiades, a cluster of stars known as the Seven Sisters."

I was covered with goose bumps. "But what's the significance of the number eight if you come from the Seven Sisters?" I asked.

"The secret is that there are not seven. There are eight. Until now, one has remained hidden. The name of the Pattern is *Kahāʻewaluiʻaʻāokalani*, the Life Force of Eight brought down to this sacred space from the heavens above."

I was as alert as he was mischievously amused.

His final words were, "Be patient. Wait and trust. More will be revealed."

Ticktock or Ticked Talk?

The Pattern was a cosmic alarm clock that had gone off in my life. However, my relationship with Steve continued ominously to ticktock away. This beating throbbed loudest in the emotional silence that gaped between us, keeping time with the sorrow beating in my heart. I knew I could not endure the sensual numbness, emotional muteness, or verbal abuse much longer. Every day I was alone became another reminder that this barely concealed time bomb was going to explode sooner or later. I knew we either had to detonate the "bomb" in a safe manner, or I would be forced to deal with a bloody mess.

By November of 1991, our relationship was at a flash point due to the fact that all nerve endings were exposed. I knew then that calling a truce was the only answer if I was to survive long enough to find answers. I asked for a separation.

I was blessed shortly after when my mother came to spend two weeks with me. During this time we crisscrossed the island, and she helped me begin to reweave the strands of my self-esteem. I was grateful for the miraculous transition we had made, from mother and daughter to genuine friends. I was thankful for her empathetic ear, unconditional love, and wholehearted support in whatever choices I made. I knew how few children ever get the loving approval from the ones they most want and need it from—their parents.

This time with my mom was the sweet and nurturing time I desperately needed. I realized that the relationship I needed to focus on was with the sacred feminine, the inner Mother. I had to do whatever was required to re-create my understanding of God and let go of old patriarchal images. It was time to find that feminine aspect of the Divine Life Force that continues to design, birth, and move the universe. Somehow I knew that only then would I more fully understand the Pattern.

As our marriage began to change, both Steve and I were aware that although we were separate, we were still jointly in the midst of a painful cycle. Whether this phase of our relationship would regenerate a sense of *we* remained to be seen. All I knew to do was breathe, inhaling acceptance and, as hard as it was, exhaling gratitude.

By spring, even as I counted my manifold blessings, I had lost hope that there was anything we could salvage in our marriage, save a friendship. Finally, we began to address the un-w-holy state of our union, and our marriage began to slide into the void. I found myself praying that our mutual pain might be dissolved.

Passing the Past

In the year since I had retrieved the Pattern, I was growing in my belief that it was also a representation of time. Since there was no beginning, middle, or end, so, too, I felt that all of life must be a continuum made up only of new nows. The Pattern helped me understand how it was that so many of my experiences could not be explained in a mentally straightforward way. I had to believe that the changes I was going through were, like my near-death experience, graduations taking me to the next cycle of this incarnation's purpose. As I began to implement these changes, I endeavored to do so with a spirit of cooperation.

That April I was in southern California, once again sitting at Lael's kitchen counter, struggling to make sense of my life. Together we kept a solemn vigil while the death knell of my marriage tolled.

While I was there, the Rodney King jury returned their verdict of "innocent" for the police officers charged in his beating. The world exploded around us. We were warned to stay home and didn't dare to challenge the infernal psychic climate by going even as far as the grocery store. For two days the media showed nothing save Los Angeles burning. I was horrified to realize that we were watching a war raging only miles away. We watched as a then nameless man was hauled from his truck, beaten, and then left for dead in the street.

What was this coverage doing to the minds and hearts of the children? What was it doing to me? How could a child feel safe in his or her home when I as an adult did not? What was this tragic episode telling the youth of our society? The world? Where was justice? What was happening to humankind?

I had resigned war a year and a half before, and now, choking on the smoke from the fires burning around us, saw that there was no way I could be a catalyst for peace if I held any anger in reserve. I had to burn all the remnants of rage, the souvenirs of war I had held on to.

I knew the Pattern of Healing was my purpose and that I was supposed to write. If this meant I was going to be a starving artist, so be it. At least I could do it in the relative peace of Hawai'i.

Wanting never to see the mainland again, I returned to the Big Island, committed to listening and writing.

Soon the busyness of my life was affecting my spirit in the same way fingernails down the blackboard pain the ears. The noise of Kailua-Kona and the hubbub of my activities were creating an internal cacophony. I could not stand it and decided I needed a retreat to finish my healing and sort out the various endings and beginnings that were happening in my life.

When I mentioned this to my friends who had introduced me to the kahuna, they told me about a Buddhist meditation center near Volcanoes National Park. I knew that any place three hours from Kailua-Kona was another world away. That afternoon I called and made a reservation to go there the following week for four days. I figured that four days would be more than enough time to cure whatever was ailing me.

Shadows in the Valley

The temple is located in the isolated Ka'ū District on the slopes of Mauna Loa, an area long ravaged by wind and fire.

I stopped to make the long drive down South Point Road and trek to the famous Green Sands Beach. On my hike, I picked up large chunks of black lava studded with olivine, a pale green crystalline stone. Arriving at the windswept beach, I watched as gusting winds sifted green silica, green and obsidian stone ground to sand by time, water, and fire.

Along the bluffs I could feel the presence of ancient spirits. Here, as on Saddle Road, I felt the presence of the ancestors as they marched beside the tumultuous sea, traversing the stone path known as the King's Trail. Like the road between the mountains, this passage inspired reverence. For a brief time I felt welcome, the wind airbrushing spontaneous memory pictures rising from my heart.

Suddenly, I was jolted out of my reverie by a whole-body sensation, a somatic response that told me I was now intruding. It was time to continue my journey.

It was late afternoon when I pulled into the small sugar-mill town of Pāhala, a sleepy little village tucked at the feet of the Nīnole Mountains. This was certainly the middle of nowhere, and I couldn't help but wonder who on earth would want to live out here, seventy miles from the nearest supermarket, movie theater, and mall.

Winding five miles up the mountain on the narrow road, I passed gargantuan cane-hauling trucks. Finally I came to Nechung Dorje Drayang Ling, the one-hundred-year-old Buddhist temple, a jewel nestled on the fringe of a pristine rain forest. When I got out of my car I was overwhelmed with the serenity that can be found only when one is virtually surrounded by ten thousand acres of silence. Standing in the most tranquil place I had ever known, I asked myself out loud, "Why do I ever want to leave this place?"

Two days later, Marya and Miguel, who have run the temple for twenty years, invited me to live there. They needed someone to help with writing their newsletters and cooking for retreats. Somehow I felt this had been planned a long, long time ago.

I moved five days later, totally at peace, knowing that this would lead to a new phase in my life. As the news of my retreat began to circulate on the coconut wireless, my friends responded identically— "Lynnclaire is moving where?" No one could believe it.

Had I given myself time to think about it, it's likely that's all I would have done—think.

The handful of friends who helped me pack (true friends, indeed)

kept telling me how brave I was. Thank goodness I didn't get what they meant.

On the morning of July 25, 1992, we piled my bedding, computer, and now greatly pared-down possessions into two cars and headed south. After lunch in Nāʻālehu, we arrived at the temple and proceeded to move my belongings into "the Pink Room," an austere twelve-by-fifteen-foot room behind the shrine in the Tara Temple. I was too blissed out to have any clue as to what I was really doing. This room was substantially smaller than the walk-in closet at the house I had been living in in Kailua-Kona. Here my closet was a thirty-inch steel bar covered by a drape.

"Uncle" Bill, a visitor from the mainland, watched with mixed amazement and hilarity as I moved in. Later that night he rechristened the Pink Room "the Rubber Room," not believing how it "stretched" to accommodate all I hauled into it.

It did not take long to realize that the path I had chosen was a decidedly isolated one.

Within a fortnight, the piece of me that was a certified human *doing* resigned. She was gone with nary a whimper. Was it possible that the part of me who quaked in her high heels whenever I came too close to the void was no longer afraid of teetering and falling off the edge into the dark?

My highest self knew that this move was the wisest thing I had done in a long while. Perhaps ever. Within weeks I began to release excess baggage at every level of my being as I saw that the things I held on to didn't keep me safe. I finally figured out what my friends meant when they said it took "courage" to make this move. It did. It was going to take more guts to stay. I could only pray this time apart would be a transition that would lead to transformation.

I soon began to appreciate the magnificent freedom that a simple life afforded me. Moving to Wood Valley was to be the first of many long lessons in nonattachment, one of the basic tenets of Buddhist philosophy.

My introduction to, and instruction in, Buddhism did not come from books or from sitting and listening to teachers. It came from being part of the temple family, from living in the community. It came from being one with the '*āina* (land). I learned as I watched how Lobzang Toldan, "Tiapala", the resident lama, lived his life. His every action, whether cutting the grass, cooking lunch, or doing morning and evening prayers, was a meditation. Tiapala is one of the kindest people I know. He is filled with gentleness, and when he laughs, you get a dose of humor as hot as the spicy curry he loves to cook.

Marya was a loving guide and often felt like a nurturing mother. She, too, truly walked the path she talked. Working with her was not only fun, it was healing.

In many ways Miguel, a peer, became a father figure of sorts. He is a master at finishing a project, only then moving on to the next one. Time and again he lovingly pushed and prodded whenever I needed to make a mental move. He led me to new levels of inner and outer silence, and soon I quit letting doors slam, turned down my music, and eventually even turned it off for long periods of time. When it came time to get down to real business, Miguel was the one who gave me a jump start.

For the first time in my life I felt free. Makeup went into a box under the bed; there was no television or radio; and when a newspaper did show up, it was usually several days old. Removed from the chaos of the "real" world, I began the process of balancing my body, mind, and spirit.

On my wall was the picture I had painted of the Pattern. At the bottom of the stairs sat the huge lava stone into which my friend Rocky had carved the Pattern for me. (Unfortunately, the interweaving was incorrect.) Every day I prayed that while I was there I would learn more of what this symbol meant. Every day I asked for divine guidance in how my purpose as a catalyst for change and love was to manifest in the world.

For months I had been grieving the closure of my marriage, and my divorce from Steve was now final. Still, no matter how right the decision to grow on separately was, I felt an emptiness that was exacerbated in the solitude. I felt a sense of loss over the fiery, but nonetheless magical, moments we had shared. In spite of the pain, I knew I would always treasure our years together and honor the healing role he played in my life.

Although I now felt that I was becoming adept at the change the Pattern reflected, I often wondered when I would ever find the love that I knew it also held.

A Baptism of Fire

One hundred days into my sabbatical from the outside world, Pele, the goddess of fire, noticed that I had moved into her neighborhood. Soon my life was turned upside down in an emotional eruption process known as "trial by fire." I was learning the hard way how unfinished business comes back around demanding resolution. I discovered that the quiet of meditation is not necessarily silence. In fact, it was where the smallest whispers and the softest cries could be heard. I could not meditate my way out of pain; rather, meditation took me more fully into it and therefore through it.

Why is it that holidays and birthdays are often painful? For me, these all come in a single season starting with my birthday and continuing through Thanksgiving, Chanukah, Christmas, New Year's, and Valentine's Day. A graph of my history would show a predictable sensory slump during this season.

The year 1992 was no exception.

As grief and loss fountained, all I knew was to hang on. I had to resist the urge to run, knowing that only when the purging of my body, mind, and soul was complete, would I see a new, though still evolving, me.

Grief as hot as Pele's lava inundated my being, and although I knew this "fire" was purifying, it hurt like hell. Remembering how I first drew the Pattern, I knew I had to embrace the nothingness and remain centered. If I was to grow in my understanding of how this pattern was a pattern of healing, I had to let it heal all kinds of relationships. My awareness expanded only when I was in an open heart space, with open hands and an open mind.

I longed to remember more of who I was. I knew that only when I ceased to forget would I stop striving to "get," no longer looking for external things or people to give me what it was I felt was lacking within myself. I knew that when my remembrance was full, I would be free *for giving*—forgiveness being the unconditional love that flows from knowing we are whole expressions of the Life Force of the universe.

While I sat in the temple doing morning and evening prayers with Tiapala, I wondered how to experience the grace that allowed the Dalai Lama to call the Chinese his greatest teachers. How was it that he was able to continually express love and compassion to those who had exiled him and his people from their land? It was in His Holiness the Dalai Lama that I first sensed the spirit of one who was truly living unconditional love.

I began to realize that I, too, needed to discover all-one-ness in the aloneness of my self-induced exile if I was to fulfill my highest purpose. The emptiness from which the Pattern emerged was now all around me. I knew that I was on an assignment to learn how to live only in the moment. The fire was further preparation, conditioning that would make me a vessel fit for sacred service.

Through my near-death experience and multidimensional deaths, I began to learn that although the body is temporary, Love is permanent. Love is the one thing in all the worlds that never perishes. Love is the lasting testament to regeneration, that which is permanently inscribed upon our minds and hearts. I knew that in spite of my pain, I was impressed with the divine mark of Love through the Pattern.

A Sequel of Grace

Grace came Thanksgiving week, a blessing arriving in the petite form of a Buddhist *rimpoche* (precious teacher) by the name of Jetsun Kushog, who came to the temple to lead a ten-day meditation retreat. Since I was not in an emotional space to be able to fully absorb her teaching, Marya and I decided that the best thing for me to do was simply to be of service. For ten days I prepared meals for the retreatants.

I knew my mind and heart were taking a turn toward healing when Jetsun honored my request for an audience. On November 20, my birthday, I was inspired by her uncomplicated approach to life and felt enveloped by her loving compassion. Although I did not feel led to "convert" to Buddhism, I did have a desire to follow in the footsteps of the Buddha. Who would not want to emulate such a life? I felt that my life would be enriched by integrating a Buddhist meditation practice into my daily spiritual life. Jetsun agreed and invited me to come for a second audience the following day.

Almost immediately I began to experience a new peace at the core of my heart. My soul came into a space of new balance. I began to find a sweet and lasting place of refuge doing a Green Tara practice—Tara being the feminine aspect of the Buddha and Green Tara signifying swift help. I began this practice praying *Om Tare Tu Tare Ture Soha*—May all I am and all I do be with loving compassion for the welfare and benefit of all sentient beings.

That day Jetsun also gave me a Tibetan name, Jamyang Odzair, meaning the feminine emanation of Manjushri, the Golden Buddha of Wisdom, one whose message is carried like a soft melody on a gentle breeze. Heaven only knows how many lifetimes it will take to live up to that name. Nonetheless, I made a vow to endeavor to live life softly while expressing my excitement, allowing nothing to diminish my awe and gratitude.

The Evolution of Remembrance

I had many intuitive knowings about the Pattern, one of the strongest being that the Sphere in the center was feminine and that it was my teacher. The center orb was like the moon; it was constant and reflective, like the earth, feminine in its essence. When I painted it, I always colored the central orb first, intuitively knowing the central Light must be brought to life before the flow and glow of the rainbow could ever be made whole. Initially, I was unable to capture the diamondlike brilliance of its core, my artistic abilities being woefully insufficient to paint the blinding hue of white-pink glowing from the center. Neither could I fully convey the essence of the Light that emanated from a Source seemingly behind the luminary Sphere. My best efforts were mediocre, as I was a dilettante with a paintbrush and could only extract the vaguest inkling of what I knew radiated from this magical orb. I captured as best I could the multifaceted incandescence of the diamond. As amethyst fire flared, this universal egg was embossed with an iridescent lightninglike latticework of gold.

Although the rings and the Sphere are separate, I realized they are w-holy interdependent, mutually responsive, both essential for the balance of the whole. I knew that out of their antipodal, yet collaborative, dance arose the harmony of paradox that gives birth to the universe, micro to macro, worlds without end.

My inner journey of remembrance that led to the retrieval of the Pattern continued to be emotionally and physically intense. The remembrance was a gift of grace, one guiding me toward the full consciousness of my suchness. Encountering the Pattern was a divine appointment, as my body, soul, and Source met at an intersection in time and space to prepare me to willingly embrace my purpose, my power. I knew my spiritual passion would only be made real in the expression of unconditional compassion.

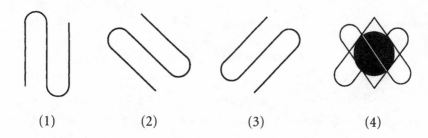

(1)   (2)   (3)   (4)

It was stunning to realize that the three-dimensional Pattern is a sine wave (1) turned ninety degrees (2 and 3) (it appears to be turned only forty-five degrees in the two-dimensional illustration above) and brought back upon itself to create a single, closed form, a simple knot (4).

In examining the human body, I knew that the two electrical transmitters were the brain and the heart, the two parts of my body most affected in the accident.

I also realized that the essence of beingness is inseparable from frequency and tone, and began to understand why music is so essential to so many people's well-being, especially my own. I thought this might also have something to do with the Music of the Spheres and might be why my hearing seemed so fine-tuned following my near-death experience. Assimilating this audible intuitive faculty into my life as a viable gift has been a long process.

It was Albert Einstein, who in many ways has been the muse of my soul these past years, who said, "Do you remember how electrical currents and unseen waves were laughed at? The knowledge about man is still in its infancy."

I believe this is one of those aspects of the Pattern where much is yet to be revealed.

But, most significantly, I saw the remembrance and retrieval of the Pattern as the link I knew would connect the pieces in my life. I knew it was the path I needed to walk in my search for Love, the meaning of life.

An acceleration along this path was just beginning.

CHAPTER TEN

Ninety Degrees and Rising

Stage Flight

*O*ne week after taking refuge with Jetsun, I began to experience powerful dreams that left what I thought had been lucid dreams in the dust. Yet for the first time, my dreams were evaporating in the warmth of the rising sun. No matter how close at hand my pencil was, the visions vaporized before I could write down my impressions. Why was this so? What did this forgetfulness signify? I again set my intention toward remembrance.

On November 28, 1992, I woke up in the middle of the night from such a dream. Only this time everything remained vivid and clear. My memory was infused with sights, sounds, smells, and voices.

In this dream I was sitting in the center of a large circle next to a blazing fire. Here I was surrounded by a group of twelve elders, six men and six women. All seemed to know me well. One was an American Indian grandmother whom I had met in meditation the previous summer. She had told me then that her name was Corvus, and we had had many dreamtime encounters. Now, standing beside the fire, she told me, "Turn the Pattern ninety degrees."

Immediately, I found I was wide awake. Absolutely certain she was in the room, I turned on the light and looked around. I was surprised to find myself alone.

"Turn the Pattern ninety degrees," I puzzled. What did she mean? I got the paper and pencil I kept near my bed for writing down my dreams and drew a line drawing of the Pattern. I turned the page sideways thinking that was ninety degrees and didn't see anything unusual.

Staring at the paper in my hand, I had a thought. Suddenly I understood what she was trying to tell me. Why hadn't I thought of this before?

I got up, found a pair of needle-nose pliers, and went to work on a wire coat hanger. She wanted me to create a three-dimensional model of the Pattern.

It took me well over an hour to get it right, and when I turned it the instructed ninety degrees, I was stunned to see the Pattern take on a totally new form. This perspective was a pentagon surround by five crescents, the sacred symbols of Islam in one form. What I also saw now were three perfectly balanced ellipses that looked for all the world like the symbol for the atom. I knew that the Pattern was powerful, and while its correspondence to this scientific cipher was shocking, it was also compelling evidence for some of my most nonrational knowings about the Pattern.

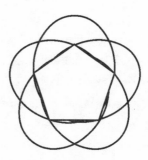

Something told me I had just made a leap in consciousness.

As I continued to contemplate this matrix, I saw that its three equal ellipses could also be symbolic of the Trinity.

Sitting there in the middle of the bed I wondered if I would ever be able to go back to sleep. Even though I'd known there were circles, I was astounded that in one simple turn, hearts forming a six-pointed star— the Star of David and the Star of Huna—became five half circles.

As I pondered this puzzle, I found myself back in the same dream state. Obviously I'd fallen suddenly asleep. I was stunned to find myself in the same place, with the same elders I'd been with earlier. However, none of them seemed at all surprised to see me.

This time Corvus was standing behind me. When she spoke, she lightly touched my left shoulder and whispered, "My child, it is time for you to remember how to fly."

Without warning, I was launched, catapulted out the end of the tunnel. As I burst out the other end, I felt like an eaglet pushed from the nest. I began to plummet, falling fast into what felt like the fathomless abyss of darkness. Once again, making a fearful descent into the unknown, I wondered if, more than when, I would hit bottom.

Then I remembered—she said I could fly!

In that instant, I began soaring through the universe. Moving as the wind, I danced with the stars. Returning again toward home, I saw the Pattern lighting the worlds. As this rainbow of pure Love floated and spun in the heavens, I moved until I saw the three circles.

Then I shot up, and flying high above the Pattern, found myself hovering, looking down on it. What I saw catapulted me back to Earth. Once more I was sitting in my bed wide awake. Still in my hand was the mangled, enamel coat-hanger model.

Sure enough. There it was. Just as I saw it when I viewed it from above, the Pattern of hearts and three circles was now the yin-yang sign. It appeared to be a single circle with the infinity sign (the number eight) in the center. It was the same when viewed from below. The Pattern was also one circle, a symbol of completion, connected by the number eight, a universal sign of prosperity and infinity.

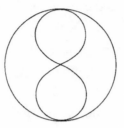

I found my brain asking, "Why have I never seen this before? Does anyone else ever remember seeing the whole thing before?"

One thought immediately came forward—*Kahāʻewaluiʻaʻāokalani*, the words of the kahuna, referring to the Pattern as the Life Force of Eight.

Investigation and Another Initiation

As 1992 slid into the past, I continued to meditate on the Pattern. Contemplating its energetic flow, I began to grow into a new understanding of Love. I began to have glimpses of what its true meaning might be in the context of a *real*ationship.

I began to see that most of my previous notions of relationship no longer fit. Even so, it was hard to let go of my old wardrobe of romantic fantasy.

During these months all kinds of circumstances dared me to clean out my inner closet. I saw that my brain was crammed with costumes that I had packed and repacked for years. I'd kept them on special hangers, never seeing that they were what kept me hung up on the past. I knew if my life was ever going to be different, or make a difference, it was time to send—for my own good will—these threadbare garments, ostentatious accessories, and flimsy trappings back to the universe for recycling.

Suddenly, I realized why it was that when I went shopping for an intimate relationship, I kept bringing home men who, in spite of external appearances, on the inside looked exactly like what was already in my closet. I realized that only when I made room in my mind and heart for a new design would the universe send one my way.

As I renewed my commitment to flow and grow with the Pattern, my true beliefs began to emerge. I saw that where I had once believed that relationships were competitive, the truth was that a *real*ationship is collaborative; where I'd once believed that relationships were to be hierarchical, the truth was that they were meant to be equitable. I saw that it was a lie that a good relationship occurs when two come together in a 50/50 deal; the truth is that both must be whole, and each must give 100 percent. I couldn't believe that I thought the best relationships were based on sensual, romantic ideals, as I discovered that the most honest and lasting *real*ationships are founded on the true intimacy of friendship. I saw that my old belief that there must be dependency, codependency, or independency was fallacious; I knew that in a healthy *real*ationship there must be an honored interdependency.

Winter eventually melted into spring, and spring flamed into the purifying fires of summer. Through the dry heat of autumn my heart was seared and my spirit left parched. The seasons of my life passed slowly as I was locked in a vacuum of inner and outer silence; all I could do was try to write my way out.

As I explored the Pattern through meditation and dreams, I learned more, but the more I learned, the more emotionally illiterate I felt. The Pattern appeared to contain many more important sacred symbols than the original three I saw in my dreams. As I worked and played with it, I began to wonder how many spiritual traditions were symbolically represented within it. This thought impelled me to research mystical, mythical, scientific, as well as sacred, symbols.

I discovered through a friend involved with the study of astrology that the Pattern was an almost precise overlay for a sixteenth-century graphic depicting the astrological chart (1).

I also discovered that the Pattern might well be a three-dimensional model for the Kabbalistic Tree of Life. Reflected within it are the pentagram, the double helix of DNA, the eight-pointed star, the Buddhist Wheel of Dharma, the ancient Sumerian symbol for "star," a symbol from the Middle Ages meaning "the family of man," the enneagram (a nine-pointed star), the star of Astarte, the Egyptian symbol for "fertility," the Egyptian symbol for "stars," the Chinese symbol for "tree," the Greek Sun Wheel, the ancient Indian symbol meaning "the family of man" and "all mankind are brothers and sisters," the butterfly, and the American Indian sign meaning "all beings friendly" (2).

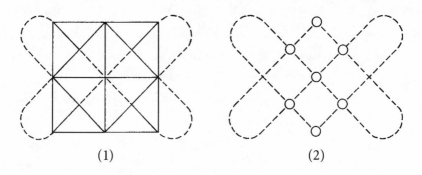

(1)   (2)

There are countless forms inherent within the Pattern, and I soon realized that I could not find a religious or cultural tradition that did not have at least one sacred symbol w-holy contained within the Pattern.

I began, somewhat hesitatingly, to share the Pattern more widely with others, asking what they felt about it. Without exception, others felt it appeared to be a universal spiritual symbol. With growing awe and wonder, I again asked the universe, "Why me?" Others were asking the same thing.

It is clear that there is nothing special about me. We are all precious and rare reflections of the Divine. I don't believe I did anything other than choose to accept a covenant with the Life Force of the universe when I made a commitment to return and be w-holy committed to sacred service.

So, here's how I began to read the possible cosmic scenario:

January 15, 1987, was the day that whatever Powers that Be decided it was time to send a message to Earth. They must have peered over the edge of Heaven to see who was in the neighborhood when they saw a golden light (the balloon) floating heavenward.

I can only imagine what they thought seeing me there, riding in that picnic basket. I can almost hear the long sigh escaping as someone muttered. "It's Lynnclaire again. What's she up to now?"

To which my Guardian Angel, anticipating a divine reprieve after thirty-five years of overtime, replied, "Oh, about seventeen thousand feet."

It must have been at that moment that the gods decided I would do as well as anyone. I can imagine the celestial gossip . . .

"Well, we'll have to help her through rehab, but at least we know that when she's back in shape, she'll talk about it."

With that, they brought me the rest of the way up, and we had that little chat. Thus, I've always considered my being the midwife to the Pattern as a kind of divine default as much as a divine order.

I finally concluded that the only answer to "Why me?" is "Why not?"

The Sun Begins to Set on the Valley

In February of 1994 I was on the island of Maui having my computer repaired when I called my friend Irv Katz to say hi. When he answered the phone, he thanked me for returning his call so quickly. I had no idea what he was talking about. He told me he had just called the Big Island and had left a message on my answering machine asking me to get right back to him. "Well. Here I am! I'm on Maui!"

Earlier that day Irv had received a call from a woman named Olivia who was visiting Hawai'i from Switzerland. They had plans to meet, and did meet, at a luncheon the following day, but he also had an intuitive hit that she and I were to meet. Thus his phone call.

He gave me her number, and an hour and a half later we met at Wailea. It was a magical connection, and we "recognized" one another immediately. Over the next couple days we spoke a lot about her work and her progress in building light centers with education, health, and retreat facilities, the Pattern, my growing sense that the time was approaching when I would be leaving the islands, and where our paths might cross again or merge.

Several days later, when I returned to the Big Island, Olivia came along. There were several people there she wanted to connect with, and as most were friends or acquaintances of mine, we continued the journey together.

One of the first stops we made was at Kealakekua Bay on the Kona coast to meet my friend, psychologist and dolphin researcher Joan Ocean. We also met Joan's friends Doug Hackett and Trish Regan. Doug and Trish had just moved to the island two weeks before and were going to be working full time with Joan.

That afternoon a small group of us sat at Joan's talking, and during this time I felt led to share the song "Embers of Starfire" with them. I didn't share the Pattern, sensing that it was not the right time.

The day Olivia left the island she presented me with a small envelope. Inside were eight one-hundred-dollar bills. "What's this?" I asked.

"It's a gift, Lynnclaire. Ask Spirit and the angels to make this money multiply, and take the Pattern to the world."

Two weeks later I met with my friend Marlene Hill, showed her the Pattern, and told her that I thought it was time to take it to the world. She agreed and wrote a check, saying, "Let's get going."

I then called Doug and Trish, this time sharing the Pattern with them. They, too, wrote a check and were directly responsible for bringing ten other people to the project.

Olivia's seed money had multiplied a hundredfold in only a month. The Pattern was on its way to the world.

Modeling Light and Love

The spring of 1994 was a busy time in Wood Valley, as His Holiness the Dalai Lama was coming to the temple for a two-day visit.

At this time, the group who had formed an organization to take the Pattern forward sent me to the mainland to meet with other interested individuals. On March 28, 1994, I left Hawai'i for San Francisco and Denver, planning to make it back to the valley just in time for His Holiness' visit.

While in the Denver area, one of the people I was meeting with voiced his thought that it would be fabulous to have a professional model maker create a prototype of the Pattern. He also thought it might be auspicious to present such a model—an original—as a gift to the Dalai Lama. He asked me, "Lynnclaire, how would you like to have a well-known, West coast graphics production company make a model?"

"Say what?"

"They're in the San Francisco Bay Area and as long as you're going to be in the neighborhood, I think maybe I could arrange for it to happen."

Given the reputation of this company, I was thrilled! I said, "You don't mean . . ."

"That's them," he replied, obviously enjoying my wonderment.

I arrived in the Bay Area Tuesday, April 5, and left a message with the contact my friend had given me. The contact called me back immediately and told me he was passing the Pattern project to one of his outside contractors. As they were swamped in house, he thought this man might have the time to do such a fast-turnaround project. He told me to expect a call from him that afternoon.

His Holiness was scheduled to make a public appearance in Wood Valley on Sunday, April 17, so time was of the essence. By midweek I still had not heard from anyone at the graphics production company and was becoming concerned.

The next morning I decided it was time to give my contact there another call. It turned out that someone had transposed the last digits of my phone number, and they had not been able to track me down. The person to whom I spoke apologized profusely and told me that apparently this meant that for whatever reason, they were meant to do the Pattern as an in-house project. He then put me through to someone else to work out the details.

After a couple minutes of conversation, he explained how swamped they were with major deadlines and said that there was just no way they could make the model in house. But then, just as if he had not heard himself speak, he asked me to bring in the artwork and a rough model that afternoon. I told him I'd be there in an hour.

When we met, he looked at my pictures of the Pattern with disbelief. He could not believe the drawings could be of the same object. However, when I pulled a crude lead model out of my purse, he got it. As intrigued as he was, he said there was no way they could do it in only five days and apologized for my having gone to the trouble of driving down.

As he attempted to hand me back the model and the artwork, I kept my hands firmly in my lap and looked him straight in the eye and said, "The part of you who told me to come down here today knew that this model was going to be made here. I'm not about to stop believing in miracles. I know there's a part of you who does, too. I don't believe it's an accident that we're sitting here. And yes, there's less than a week, but we both believe it can be done! I know that if you ask, someone here is going to know that this project is theirs."

He cracked a smile. "Okay. No promises, but I'll see what I can do."

As I walked out the door, I knew in my mind and heart that the job was done.

Twenty Monks and Two Million Mantras

When I left, he took my unrefined lead model of the Pattern and the pictures and walked into a room that was filled with model engineers, all working on various projects. He called for their attention.

One of them—who in my mind and heart will always be the Grand Wizard of model making—later told me that when he looked up and saw the model, he wanted to run up and grab it out of his supervisor's hands.

When the supervisor said, "I just met a woman named Lynnclaire, and I wonder if there is anyone here who has any feelings about Tibetan Buddhism," the Grand Wizard said he expected every hand in the room to go up. But he alone was on his feet, frantically waving his arms.

He listened as the supervisor told him the story. He knew this was his project, and the supervisor handed him the model, the pictures, and my phone number.

We spoke the next day and arranged to meet Sunday.

When we met, his intuitive knowing and eagerness matched my enthusiasm. His girlfriend told us that her sister was doing graduate work in Buddhist studies at Harvard and asked if it would be appropriate to send copies of the Pattern to the monks there. She wanted to ask them for prayers, knowing that the model would be presented as a gift to the Dalai Lama. I assured her that it would be more than appropriate; it would be a blessing.

The Grand Wizard understood the deadline, and we all knew he would be sleep deprived to accomplish the project. Nonetheless, he made the commitment and agreed to have the model delivered to United Airlines at San Francisco airport by 6:00 A.M. Saturday. I would pick it up in Kailua-Kona when it arrived several hours later.

The Nechung Medium

I returned to the island to face a busy week as everyone braced for the massive influx of people who would be coming into the valley. Meanwhile I was packing to move to California. I was astounded to realize how much stuff I had managed to accumulate in two years.

Two years? How was it possible?

On several occasions during the final week at the temple I was honored to spend time with the group of monks who had arrived in advance of His Holiness to prepare for his arrival. This included several hours of personal time with the Nechung Medium, the monk who for the past eight years had been the trance medium for an entity who has guided the Tibetan people for centuries.

During our visits, we talked at length about the Pattern, a number of the pieces I'd written concerning it, as well as many of my nonrational experiences. This gentle monk was able to help me understand the spiritual implications of these experiences as no one had before. He reassured me that I was truly "on purpose" and fulfilling a commitment I had made in a prior incarnation. He told me that to be allowed to choose to come back on that cold February night in 1987 was most auspicious. He told me that to be entrusted to bring back a treasure from the other side was a high honor. He also made it very clear that, yes, it was time for me to leave the valley and take its message of healing and Oneness to the world.

More Magic

Saturday morning arrived, and just before Doug and Trish and I headed for Kona to meet the flight to pick up the model of the Pattern, the Grand Wizard called to let us know it was on its way, as well as to tell us the rest of the story.

He first decided to construct the external rings of the Pattern from solid, quarter-inch-square copper. He then decided to use a Lucite amethyst sphere in the center, and on Monday he sourced it from a local manufacturer. His plan was to pick it up Friday on his lunch break, hoping that the paint would be dry enough for him to insert it that evening.

Friday, he left to pick up the sphere and was stunned when he arrived to find a sign on the front door reading, "Closed for retooling. Will open in two weeks."

He returned to his workplace to contemplate his options. He had never made a Lucite sphere but knew he could if he had to. But he also knew it would take at least eight hours—eight hours he didn't have. Sitting at his desk considering his alternatives, he had asked for divine help when he heard someone walk into the shop. He lifted his head to see one of his coworkers standing in front of him with an unusual look on his face.

The man asked, "By any chance do you need this?" In his hand was a Lucite sphere, the exact size and color needed to complete the Pattern.

"How did you know?" the Grand Wizard asked. "Where did you get it?"

"Well, believe it or not, this has been sitting on my desk for three years. I just always left it there figuring that someday someone might need it."

"But how did you know I needed it now?"

"Well, this may sound crazy . . . but would you believe it told me?"

The Grand Wizard then put his girlfriend on the phone. She relayed the message from her sister that the monks at Harvard had each done 100,000 mantras to remove all obstacles and had included the Pattern in this ceremony as this gem made its way to the Dalai Lama. She also told me they had packed the Pattern in paper on which the mantra had been written.

Reunion

The flight was on time and as soon as the luggage arrived, I saw an agent with the box.

"If he only knew what he has in his hands," I thought.

The box itself was another labor of love, a gift from one of the men at the graphics production company who spent his Friday evening designing and making a custom container for the Pattern.

I could hardly imagine what it would be like to see the Pattern three dimensionally, let alone hold it in my hands. I was trembling as I picked up the box, and we went to sit on a stone wall where we could be out of the crush of people.

Trish sat behind me while Doug focused the camera.

Words failed all of us when I opened the box and the first thing we saw was the mantra the monks at Harvard had been doing all week. There on the top were written the words, "Om Tare Tu Tare Ture So Ha." It was the same mantra I had been doing hundreds of times every day for a year and a half!

Again, I felt we were being given a powerful reminder of our responsibility to the universe regarding the Pattern. "May all I am and all I do be with loving compassion for the welfare and benefit of all sentient beings."

I knew that the Pattern was a global trust, and we were charged with its stewardship.

Without a doubt, a mighty throng of angels surrounded this matrix of healing, the Pattern that the heavenly hosts determined was now ready to be revealed.

Returning to the temple that afternoon, I again met with the Nechung Medium to show him the model. To my wonderment, he asked to keep my original artwork, my drawings of the Pattern. The little voice in my heart whispered, "Nonattachment, Lynnclaire." Actually, I think I was more embarrassed than attached.

Showers of Blessings

Everything was ready and all we could do was pray it did not rain.

The morning of April 17, 1994, dawned bright and sunny. By 10:00 A.M. the road into the valley was closed. When the temple grounds opened at noon, people began to flood into the valley on foot. It was an amazing sight, and the love and courtesy extended by one and all were inspiring.

When His Holiness came onto the front lanai of the temple to take his seat on the dais, there was utter silence. And then he chuckled! It was one of the most magical moments of lightness I have ever experienced.

His Holiness had been speaking for less than an hour when the clouds began to gather as they tend to do on the edge of the rain forest. Within minutes a soft mist was falling, yet no one moved. His Holiness continued to speak, changing from Tibetan to English. Within a few minutes a steady rain was falling and still no one moved. As His Holiness shared simple words of wisdom you could feel his loving compassion. We were now drenched.

I believe every person's spirit was touched that day by the essence of this man who calls himself "a simple monk . . . one who is honored to serve all sentient beings."

I had thought I would be able to present the model of the Pattern to His Holiness during a public audience, but this turned out not to be possible.

It didn't matter. I felt wrapped in grace and knew at the level of my soul that this, too, was Divine Order. I realized how I had grown into a place of surrender and found myself in a cocoon of nonattachment. I saw how all along Spirit had intended my connection to be with the Medium. That afternoon he told me he would be the one presenting the model and the artwork to the Dalai Lama. He also told me he would look forward to welcoming me home when I visited Dharamsala. Soon.

My heart was filled to overflowing with love, awe, and gratitude.

A New Day Dawning

People often ask how it felt to spend two years living in relative isolation, seventy miles from nowhere. (I remind them that the real thrill was living on top of Kīlauea, the world's most active volcano. I am always amused when people say they cannot imagine why anyone would choose to live so remotely, let alone near a volcano. Obviously, they have never been there.)

It was a gift to be allowed to go into the silence of my soul.

Here the universe reminded me to preserve the beauty, tranquillity, solitude, and essence of this planet, as well as discover the serenity within myself.

As I looked back at my two years in Wood Valley, I realized what an incredible measure of grace was mine. While I endured a period of aloneness and loneliness, I was no longer afraid of the silence. I was no longer afraid of the dark, and my vision transcended what I saw with my eyes.

In the shadow of Mauna Loa I witnessed the death and dying of many of my old patterns. Through absolutely amazing grace, I was permitted to be the loving midwife at the rebirth of yet another new me. (How many incarnations do we get in one body?) Here I learned that even though the world would shake, rattle, and roll around me—even under me—I could focus my intention and tap into a deep reservoir of abiding calm. I discovered w-holy-ness, learning that stillness is often what connects us with the Divine. In a state of remembrance with our all-one-ness, I found the power of co-creation.

In many ways, these months were a pilgrimage through the valley of the shadow of death. I knew that as I moved closer to the Light the shadows—my own—would loom larger than ever. But I also saw that the shadows—dark places where fears breed and illusions take root—

are always behind us, in that place we call "the past." I saw that when our attention remains focused on the Light of Love that is before us in the now, we are free to progress. I also realized that the future is never in my hands. I can only anticipate it by living fully, here and now. If I invest energy into expecting anything from tomorrow or someone else, I am setting myself up for an "inside job" of premeditated resentment.

The valley was empty that Tuesday morning, April 19, 1994, as I prepared to leave, escorted by the Nechung Medium. I realized that a new pattern, the Pattern of Healing, was indeed on its way to the world.

C H A P T E R   E L E V E N

A Brief Anthology of Magical Moments

Weaving the Strands of Light and Love

*I*n the twenty-four months since my exodus from the valley, literally hundreds of magical stories have been "written" in my book of Life. It seems that every day the Pattern is the catalyst for new synchronicities. It has a special way of reviving soulular remembrances and bringing about heartfelt reunions. For some it has been the impulse to begin a new phase of life, a guide on an inner- and interdimensional progression of purpose. For others it has brought inner peace when the universe decreed that their physical sojourn was over and has served as a bridge over which their spirit was carried "home."

Living intimately with the complex dynamic simplicity of the Pattern has helped me understand the vital continuum of change. It has helped me mentally untangle many of the common, but snarly, knots that bound me. As a result, it has freed me to form powerful bonds, connections of heart and soul that transcend physical proximity.

Certainly, there have been days where I was—am—required to braid the sensible with the absurd. I've learned that although the logical and the mystical may appear to be contradictory, they are both essential to understanding and balancing. Living in the midst of immense global change, I have learned the importance of staying centered. There have been times that required no less than the moment-by-moment renewal of my faith.

But those who have shared the incredible journey that now has you reading the words on this page will tell you it has been quite a trip! Admittedly, the biggest lesson we've all learned has been the one that required the surrender of all attachment to a particular outcome, most notably the abandonment of any and all preconceived thoughts as to the Pattern's "due date."

Well, it's here now! And one thing we can all certainly attest to is that we are living a genuine, never-ending story!

In these closing pages, I'd like to share several of the inspiring incidents that have happened along the way. These are the connections that were the buoys that kept me—body, mind, and heart—afloat when I felt I might drown in an ocean of doubt. Interspersed throughout these anecdotes are thoughts and heart impressions about the Pattern. We—I and those with whom I am blessed to share this mission of Wonder—look forward to hearing yours!

A White Buffalo

In late August of 1994 one of my board members and I were en route to a business meeting, traveling up the northern California coast.

We'd left my home early that morning in order to make a brief stop at a gem shop I'd discovered some weeks earlier. I wanted to show my friend a stone I'd found that I felt was somehow connected with the Pattern. We had a nice visit with the owner and bought several pieces before continuing north.

We arrived at Nancy's, our final destination, and had not been there long when incredible synchronicities began to occur. Soon it was obvious to everyone that Someone else had determined our agenda in advance. What was unfolding and eventually transpired appeared to have nothing to do with the original purpose of the meeting.

Actually, the connection began two years before.

Since March of 1992, I've been having a recurring, evolving dream that has to do with, among other things, Mt. Rainier and American Indians. The most recent turn within the dream was so strong and specific that I knew I was to be on the mountain at a specific date, at a specific time. For what reason, I had no idea, but the knowing was so deeply incontestable that I had reserved the ticket. Furthermore, I had contacted my sister Katie, feeling that she was to be with me. We made plans to camp out on the mountain, since neither of us had the budget for a hotel. This, in spite of the fact that we knew it was likely to be freezing that high on the mountain.

During the course of that meeting, Nancy and I found out we both originated in the Northwest, and I mentioned my pending trip to Seattle. It turned out that she, too, was going to the Seattle area to attend a social event. Not only was she going on the same day, but we were booked on the same flight. When she invited me to stay with her at her family's home, I welcomed the opportunity!

When she asked me why I was going, I briefly told her about my dream and the particular night I was to spend on the mountain. I also mentioned that the dream had led me to anticipate making a connection with the American Indians, specifically the elders.

The funniest look spread across Nancy's face and I knew something was up. She then walked us to a door leading to a terrace overlooking the ocean, a deck we had not been able to see from where we were sitting. There in meditation was a man who was obviously an American Indian. When Nancy opened the door, he looked up, and she invited him to join us.

She then introduced us to her house guest, an Apache shaman.

I clearly recall the look on his face when he first saw the Pattern. I can also see the look that came into his eyes when he shared his remembrance of it. While in deep meditation and on vision quests he had seen flashes of rainbow light that he now knew could only be the Pattern. He was amazed to finally see it in its entirety.

He then asked me exactly how I believed the Pattern was significant to his people. Out of my mouth came a reply that surprised us all.

"This Pattern has deep meaning to your people. I believe it is related to the birth of a white buffalo."

I was almost embarrassed for saying this, as I had absolutely no idea where this thought came from or what it meant. The only white buffalo I'd ever heard of was the name of a woman in a song.

He, however, knew exactly what this meant. He proceeded to tell us that the birth of a white buffalo was a prophecy that had been given and passed down for more than five hundred years among American Indian tribes. He shared that the elders had long spoken of this event and of their belief that when this vision was fulfilled the world would soon usher in a new and lasting era of peace.

Later that afternoon as we were preparing to leave, he took us outside to show us his medicine stick, a spiritual wand he created to use in sacred rituals. There, prominently displayed, was this same, very rare stone that I had looked at and purchased earlier that day. Cosmic mischief, for sure.

The following week Nancy and I went to Seattle. When my sister and I went to the Office of Indian Affairs, we discovered the office was closed. It was a state holiday in honor of American Indians. On the bulletin board we found out that one of the big events was a powwow that night at the Seattle Center. We went and experienced a string of magical moments, most notably in the simple interactions with the children sitting near us.

That night Nancy attended her social event, where she reconnected with friends. When she returned, she told us there was one couple in particular she had a feeling we were to meet with, and following her feeling she had made plans for us to get together the next day.

The meeting went all over the cosmic map! Showing her friends the Pattern led to sharing the details of the trip's origin. Upon hearing that I was guided to spend the night on the mountain, one friend asked, "I'd love to join you. How would you like to stay at my family's home on the mountain?" She then told us of a magnificent piece of property high on the side of Mt. Rainier that her family had owned since the turn of the century.

We spent a magical day and night on the mountain. Instead of camping in the freezing cold, we cozied up in a well-maintained cabin overflowing with generations of memories—and with hot showers, no less!

No less astounding an "ordinary" was that only weeks later the white buffalo was born, making headlines around the world.

The Pattern as a uniting symbol has the potential to bridge the oceans of the heart, bringing together diverse cultures in a fundamental way. The Pattern's message is that of Love, compassion being the nexus over which abundance streams from Heaven to Earth. May this Pattern be a rainbow of hope, bringing all corners of the world into a circle of peace.

Crossing Grace

In September of 1994, immediately following my return from Mt. Rainier, the progression of knowings continued. One of the first was that I would be moving right after Thanksgiving. Where I would be moving to, I didn't have a clue. But my knowing was so absolute that I gave my notice to my landlord.

At this time I also followed up on another one of those erstwhile, fuzzy connections that sometimes come in lucid dreamtime. It had been hanging around for months, since the morning I had awakened with a thrumming query ricocheting through my brain, "Borey-who?"

I had no idea what it meant and wondered first if these might not be Hebrew words. But one day when a friend mentioned a woman by the name of Joan Borysenko, I got one of those cosmic "Aha's!" Hmmmm . . . maybe, just maybe, "Borey-who" wasn't a what, but a who—a Bory-senko who! A rabbi friend told me that, interestingly enough, "Bory hu" translates to "he who heals."

Discovering that Joan was, among other things, cofounder of the Mind Body Health Clinic at Harvard's Deaconess Hospital, I knew I was on to something. I tracked down her phone number, called, and learned from her assistant that she was on a speaking tour and would not return for a month. I left my name and phone number and said I would call again.

A month later I returned home late one evening and found a message on my answering machine from Joan Borysenko. She was returning my call and asked that I call her back. Since it was after midnight in Boulder, I knew I had to wait until morning.

I had a hard time sleeping that night and finally gave up and got up at five. I kept feeling that I was supposed to call, even though I knew full well that six in the morning was too early to call even my mother. Something was up here . . .

Finally, at six my time, seven mountain time, I said—"That's it. I'm calling."

I dialed Joan's number and was surprised that she immediately answered and was relieved that she sounded wide awake. I identified myself, and before I could even tell her why I was calling, she wanted to tell me why she'd called.

After being on the road for weeks, Joan returned home the day before to her mountain sanctuary. Upon walking into her office she found her in-box jammed with, literally, three hundred pink slips, all calls waiting to be returned. Picking up the stack, she was heading upstairs when one of the slips fluttered to the floor.

Now, Joan and I are alike in that neither of us sees even the smallest of things as accidents. So, curious to see who was trying to get her attention, she picked it up to check it out. On it was a name she'd never heard, and a phone number in an area code she was not familiar with. Me.

Immediately she called, and after one round of phone tag here we were.

She then passed the "talking stick" back, and I gave the "nickel" version of the Pattern story. I was not two minutes into it when Joan reclaimed the stick. We were about to find out that we didn't really need a phone for our connection!

Joan had woken up at 4:00 A.M. that morning with a knowing so sure that she woke up her husband and began bending his ear. To his sleepy exasperation, she kept talking, and when the phone rang three hours later, was still talking—about a symbol, a pattern she knew was going to unite the world.

Hello?

Isn't it great when the universe—God—Goddess—Angels—Great Spirit—the One—whoever—sends us these fabulous wake-up calls? I've learned that it is wise to pay attention when we sense that "call" coming in, even when it comes in the middle of the night, or when, as sometimes happens, we suspect the call may be collect.

Three weeks later Joan and I met in Boulder and began what continues to be a magical journey. It is an extraordinary continuation of what has, in many ways, become a waking dream.

Just as I had known from my dream, within a matter of weeks Joan invited me to move to Colorado and share her home. Together we lived in the mountains beside the Continental Divide, sharing what for both of us was a profound winter of change. They were days of wading with a friend across fast-flowing rivers of grace. By infinite mercy and divine benevolence we would together safely make it to the other side of our mutual transitions.

Rafie's Stars

Since my near-death experience, I have felt called to work extensively with people who are in major life transitions and are preparing for transformation—especially with those facing death, both patient and family. While living in Boulder, I worked with individuals who had been referred to me by Joan, as well as others.

In late January I received a call from Dr. Joel Miller, a Denver psychiatrist. He called me after hearing that I had worked with a friend and colleague of his.

Within hours, I was in Denver meeting with him and his wife, Susan—also known as Rafie, short for Raphael, the Archangel of Healing. Although her body was ravaged by amyotrophic lateral sclerosis, also known as Lou Gehrig's disease, and a twenty-year battle with cancer, it was obvious that Rafie wanted to heal the wounds to her heart and soul and wanted to be cured. In spite of the devastating effects of disease, everyone knew Rafie would never give up her love of life. Her spiritual health and humor were whole, but her fear of death was tenacious. This irreducible fear was offset only by her equally dynamic belief in the healing power of love and the reality of angels, miracles, and magic.

Rafie and I bonded that night in a powerful way. When she saw the Pattern, something she had forgotten awakened in her. When she saw that I held no fear of death—which was what she feared more than anything else—she was willing to remember that which she had repressed, old stuff that was making her "sick at heart." In spite of the fact that I could promise healing but not a cure, it became clear that it wasn't a matter of IF we were going to work together, for in Rafie's mind there was only one question—"When?" She wanted me to stay, then and there. However, there was a lot of divine preparation to be done!

Over the next seven months I spent many weeks with Rafie and her family. This time was an incredible gift, providing me with many lessons I needed to learn in order to come to a deeper understanding of my purpose as well as to continue my own healing.

It was Rafie who first noticed that, as a three-dimensional model of the Pattern spun, an unusual phenomenon occurred. In motion, the Pattern took on an altogether different form. It looked like a rectangle, with a pyramid reflected above and below. In the center of this rectangle flashed three white, laserlike stars, and straight through the center a single line of light connected the apex and nadir points of the pyramids. Since that day, I and others have referred to this phenomenon as "Rafie's Stars."

Rafie, like the Pattern, taught me that focus is one of the most powerful life-sustaining generators of love. When the impulses of passion and compassion are unified, they spark within the mind and heart an almost electrical connection with the Source of the universe. Working with Rafie and the Pattern, we brought a new clarity to communication and began to balance rational discourse with compassionate hearing. She was my teacher, showing me that speech and silence are both crucial elements in the dynamic dance of healing.

Within weeks of our meeting, Rafie's speech was gone, and communication was done on a tool known as "the Board." This is a clear Lucite sheet, on both sides of which appear basic words and the alphabet. Rafie would look at the word or letter she wanted, then look at you, spelling out whatever she wanted to say. The person holding the Board became Rafie's mouthpiece and was obliged both to answer and to say whatever she spelled.

As a testament to the "Susan" piece of her personality there was a line on the board that I referred to as "the Blue Line." This row of words held all of her favorite swear words! When Rafie was mad, everyone knew it, and she used this line to turn the air blue! It didn't matter if it was against your "religion" to swear—if you were holding the Board, you got to channel Rafie's wrath. If you weren't swearing loud enough, she also let you know! Oh, the woe that befell one soul when Rafie discovered that that same someone had removed the Blue Line from her board . . . Suffice it to say the words were quickly replaced!

Rafie's unfailing sense of humor and walloping dose of "piss and vinegar" taught me anew to appreciate life and grab all the juicy moments and squeeze every last drop of joy out of them!

I will never forget one cool August night . . .

Before going to bed that night, Rafie extracted the promise (she was so good at that!) that at 2:00 A.M. we would get her up to watch a predicted meteor shower. This meant dressing her—which was not an easy task under her "normal" circumstances—then wheeling her and all her medical support paraphernalia out to the middle of the street where we would have a clear view of the heavens. We managed, never mind that no one, save Rafie, was even half awake.

For half an hour we sat in the chilly mountain air where there was a lot more waiting going on than there was watching of any meteors. But I remembered that prayer takes many forms, and that night we prayed some unusual prayers! One might imagine what a sleepwalking neighbor or community patrol car might have thought had they cruised into the cul-de-sac in the wee, predawn hours, where, with our eyes glued to the heavens, we sang "Twinkle Twinkle Little Star," "Rocky Mountain High," and "When You Wish upon a Star!" We were begging those meteors to dance a little lower, and dance they did! Although she was unable to speak, none of us will ever forget the enchanting sound of Rafie's squeal when she caught sight of her first shooting star. We all were transported as we watched it blaze across the heavens high above Denver. Doubtless, we entertained—or were entertained by—angels that night.

Every day, in spite of the bitter pill of pain, laughter was Rafie's favorite prescription for healing. One of her preferred remedies was to ask one of her angelic care givers to entertain the troops with a rousing bout of dirty dancing. In truth, it was a command performance. Rafie would order that Whitney Houston's "I Want to Dance with Somebody" be cranked to the max, and we would howl with laughter as her care giver would bump and grind the dance she'd been paid to perform twenty years and twenty pounds before as a go-go dancer.

Yet, as weeks went on, Rafie and I knew we were moving closer to our ultimate purpose—to assist one another in fully releasing fear and remembering how to return to love; how to die. The Pattern brought both of us an amazing measure of peace, and she never removed the pendant of the Pattern I had had made for her. For months, everyone—the kids and nurse's aides, one and all—were also wearing them.

On September 26, I returned to Denver, after not having seen Rafie for three weeks. When I walked into her room I was shocked by the change those short weeks had made. Virtually gone was her ability to make a facial expression; her face was now carved with pain. I walked to her bedside, wrapped my left arm around her fragile body and put my right hand on her heart, tucking her as close to my heart as we could get without pain. Almost immediately, she fell asleep. Her care giver was stunned, as Rafie had not slept in two days—so great was her fear of not waking up or choking.

She slept for an hour, and when she woke up, we knew it was time to talk. The only thing tethering Rafie to the planet was her fear. Over the next twenty-four hours, we began to slice through the illusions that bound her to pain and to her body, as love gave her the strength to remember the rainbow promise of Light and Love.

On September 27, 1995, my dear friend Susan "Rafie" Miller, surrounded by her family, crossed from her pain into the full remembrance of joy. I was blessed to be there, keeping the original promise she had extracted months before, my hands on her heart, as she made the transition to the next stage of her soul's journey.

We are all surrounded by divinely appointed attendants like Rafie, individuals and angels whose purpose is to remind us of our manifold blessings. They are in our lives to administer our daily generous portions of love—love that, if we are willing and free to receive it, will be pressed down and poured out to overflowing.

As we celebrate life with love and thanksgiving, a song of celestial rapture fills the firmament. It is the vibration of the angels' chorus that is carried on stardust, a rhapsody kindred to our own heart song. For both Rafie and me, the Pattern was the catalyst for this angelic aria. It sparked within us an electrical surge of miraculous power, energy that is held at the nucleus of our being.

When we open our heart and release our fears, we soar into the joy of full aliveness. Here we are free to dance in that sacred space—both here and there—where with others we can bask in the wonder of being spiritually whole. Luxuriating in the awe of the All and the I Am, we are all assistants of mercy, each of us a catalyst for love. We have all, in spite of our occasions of pain and sorrow, flourished in the refining of our hearts.

When a door opens and the universe leads us in a transition of change, be it death, divorce, or geography—anything that affects our inner or external worlds—we must be willing to go through it. On the other side is the next phase of our divinely inspired purpose. No matter where it takes us, we can know that the hour is appointed, and our soul has been anointed, ordained, and fully prepared.

When we intentionally step forward into our purpose, when intuition and the innate intelligence of the heart are honored, doors open magically and without fear we can cross to the other side.

Fly high, Angel Rafie!

An Angel's Prayer

For one moment, imagine,
A place where you are safe,
Where strength will guide you on your way.
Close your eyes now, imagine,
Hope is all around.

These are my prayers for you:
May your spirit always shine,
May happiness fill your days to come,
May your journey lead you through
A path that's filled with peace.
These are my prayers for you.

Hold my hand now, imagine,
Together we will search
And find comfort along the way.
I will always be beside you,
Together let us dream.

There is a time and place for answers.
For now release your soul and see,
The light within your heart is free,
To lead you to the place
Where you will find your peace.

Now it's time to start believing.
Allow your faith to soar with the angels of Shechinah.
They will bless each day with wonder,
Allow their wings to wrap around you, protect you.

These are my prayers for you,
May your spirit always shine,
May happiness fill your days to come,
May your journey lead you through
A path that's filled with peace.
These are my prayers for you.

Written by Tami Miller for her mother, Susan Rafie Miller

Angels in Real Time

On April 28, 1995, while I was having major dental work done, something went very seriously wrong.

Earlier that morning I had been put on alert, my intuition yelling, "Heads up!" This is the phrase that was the customary, howbeit unorthodox, inner S.O.S. that without fail alerts me that a lesson is forthcoming. Thus put on notice, I asked a friend to stay with me and hold my feet during the procedure, extracting the promise that no matter what, he would not let go. This way, I knew if something went wrong, I would not be able to leave my body—at least not easily.

Only moments after the doctor injected the area around the surgical site I was out of body—save my feet. I was sitting upright and looking directly in my friend's face. At the time, no one yet knew that the anesthetic had gone directly into a rogue blood vessel, mainlined straight to my brain.

I turned to look over my right shoulder at my body lying in the chair, and heard the doctor tell me to open my mouth and tilt my head back. Oblivious to my nonresponse, he opened my mouth wider, and with his thumb on my teeth, he pushed my head back. At the same time, I accurately "read" both my blood pressure and pulse—b/p 54/25, pulse 12 and falling fast. This was not good news. I knew that if someone didn't wake up and pay attention very quickly, I was on my way home in spite of the promise I had made to stick around.

With that in my mind, I turned back to my friend and "shouted" as loud as I could to try and get his attention. "Are you going to notice what's going on?" I screamed. The second time I "yelled," somehow something registered.

Relieved, I heard him call my name, and as the room erupted into pandemonium I laid back down into my body. It wasn't easy. In fact, it was like getting pulled through a keyhole.

Several hours later, I experienced what I believe was the real reason for this episode. I was lying in a recovery room, when in the left-hand corner of the room I saw two incredible beings. I had no doubt that these were angels. One was a huge, powerful presence whose countenance was bluish (I'm serious) and whose essence was filled with the most amazing compassion. I believed that angels were supposed to be androgynous, but this being was very masculine. Next to him was another angel, more human-sized and golden in tone. I recognized him as my overworked Guardian Angel—frustrated, I'm sure, at having to call in oversized divine assistance in order to get my attention.

Flat on my back, forced to look up, I heard the bluish angel ask, "Lynnclaire, if you were given the opportunity to share only one truth with the world—such that upon hearing that one truth, those who heard it would not just know it, they would believe it—what would that message be?"

It somehow registered somewhere inside me that *knowing* is static information contained only in the brain, but *believing* is the dynamic that happens when data take root in the heart and a new understanding blossoms into life-changing wisdom.

Suddenly, everything became crystal clear, and my answer was simple: I answered aloud, "That we are lovable."

Upon hearing my response, the angels left the room and I turned to my friend. Hypersensitive to all kinds of energy, he had been well aware of an energetic charge zinging in the room. I shared what had just happened, and in that moment I knew that if every soul truly believed he or she were lovable we would have peace on Earth.

Both the Pattern and you and I are on this earth for this, our highest soul purpose. May it be so.

The Nexus for a New Generation

The summer of 1995, as a result of my friendship with the Miller family, I had the privilege of sharing a week with twenty-six young Israeli and Palestinian women, aged fourteen to eighteen. They had come together for the express purpose of finding a common bond, bringing with them a commitment to lay down—if only for a short time—their culturally and religiously inculcated abhorrence for one another. Although this mistrust was ingrained in their souls on a cellular and soulular level, they were dedicated to finding a shared vision, or to constructing a new one they themselves would design from the unique perspective of the feminine.

Only hours before my flight to join them, I caught a news bulletin on the radio announcing that there had been yet another breach in the Middle East peace accord. A Palestinian faction had already taken the credit for the bombing of an Israeli bus that killed five college students and injured more than one hundred. I could only pray, not daring to imagine what the atmosphere would be like among the girls when I arrived.

In that moment I resolved to be only a clear light shining in what was, at that moment, a dimmed world. I knew all I could be was an example of unconditional love, and all I could do was help create a safe place.

As timing would have it, Mother Nature was orchestrating a thunderstorm when I arrived, the weather on the mountain matching the infernal emotional climate inside. Even then the press was waiting for a statement from these young women on the tragedy. My heart opened and tears flowed as I observed their struggle to put together a unified statement. In observing them, I understood how the sins of one generation visit the next.

These young women were children who in many ways had been robbed of their innocence. On many levels they were compelled to wear the psychic demeanor of adults, forced to exist in a world where political expediency and religious mandates combined to create wholesale chaos.

Over the course of a week I shared the different perspectives of the Pattern with these young women. The Jewish girls saw the Star of David in the Heart of Intimacy perspective. The Palestinians saw their sacred symbol, the Crescent, in the Nucleus perspective. A Palestinian Christian saw the cross in the Flower of Life perspective. Each initially saw only *her* perspective. Asked to identify the common aspects, they acknowledged its rainbow essence, as well as the center Sphere. Each of their traditions held similar beliefs and mythologies about the rainbow and the circle.

When I asked if all these symbols might be the same thing, the response was emphatic and universal: "No way."

Only when they saw the large model and saw the whole did they realize that each of their viewpoints was valid, but that it was just one perspective of the larger Truth. Even in our differences we are connected by that which is, at its essence, essentially the Same.

That week I witnessed individual miracles as I saw beautiful young women come to a place of remembrance of their Goddessential being. I was touched by their love and curiosity, and their willingness to grow and change. Each had a desire to become an ember of light in a very challenged corner of the world. I watched as these incredible young women discovered and honored a new piece of themselves during their time together. I observed with admiration as they came to realize that only if they were at ease with themselves could they hear one another and find a mutual peace.

That week the girls became the co-creators of peace on that piece of earth atop that mountain. They realized that only as they met each other at the heart would they be able to create a new space for empathy in their lives and equanimity in their homeland.

It was wondrous to witness as they designed a communication infrastructure for themselves and, indeed, their generation. Hour by hour, day by day, they began to lay the foundation for an ongoing dialogue, a bedrock on which they could build a new and fragile bridge for peace. Their common prayer was that in the next millennium their bond might prove to be a strong and sturdy nexus of respect.

Only if we project love into each new *now* will the next generation know peace. No longer can the planet afford for the legacy of war and guilt to be passed on. It is up to us whether or not our children and our children's children will be forced to revisit our most elementary school, the school of suffering. This is a mental institution where shame, humiliation, blame, condemnation, regret, excuses, and heartache have been and always will be the loudest and most strident tutors.

May we listen and hear the wisdom of the children. May we remember that even the smallest child is a progenitor of grace, one who, with infinite simplicity, can unravel and reveal the most complex truth.

The Reunion of Science, Heart, and Mind

On January 12, 1996, the *Wall Street Journal* ran an article entitled "The Spirit in Technology" by Tom Mahon. Because its content so strongly related to the message and truth of the Pattern, I wanted very much to include it in this book. Doing so, however, would require permission from Mr. Mahon, and his byline identified him only as a San Francisco–based writer.

For two days, I made countless calls to the newspaper trying to track down Mr. Mahon, but every call led nowhere. No one in a *Wall Street Journal* office anywhere—New York, San Francisco, or the other area codes to which I was directed—could tell me where the article came from or who Tom Mahon was. The science editor had never heard of him. Neither had the religion editor. And so it went.

When it came time to turn in the manuscript and Mr. Mahon was still nowhere to be found, I had no choice but to omit his article from the book. That is, until my phone rang. From the other end of the line came the words, "Lynnclaire, this is a voice from your past. You may not remember me, but we met on a plane almost two years ago." Of course, I remembered. My friend went on to tell me that just recently, while flying to the East Coast, his flight had developed serious difficulties, and passengers had been prepared for a crash landing. He told me that as he sat there with his head between his knees and his arms over his head, he recalled our conversation about my near-death experience and the Pattern, and he knew that—whatever happened—it was going to be alright. He vowed in that moment that if he lived through the landing, he would track me down and call me.

We had a wonderful talk, and since he is in the publishing business, in the course of the conversation I mentioned my situation in regard to Mr. Mahon. He said, "Lynnclaire, I have some friends at the *Wall Street Journal.* Give me some time, and let's see what I can do." Not an hour had passed when the phone rang again and my friend boomed, "I found him!" An hour later Mr. Mahon called. We shared information about our life paths and are planning to meet in person!

I am awed, as always, by the synchronicity of these events, touched by the depth of connection established in just a few short hours, and blessed to share Tom Mahon's article with you.

The Spirit in Technology

BY TOM MAHON

Coincidentally or not, our nation's spiritual crisis has paralleled a remarkable explosion in technical prowess. As one raised in a traditional faith who has spent twenty-five years writing about electronic, atomic, and genetic engineering, I would like to offer an observation about the connection between the two fields.

We are the first generation to experience the full effects of the three centuries–old decoupling of the physical landscape (as understood by science, manipulated by technology, and capitalized on by business) from the moral landscape (as taught by our religious institutions). It's little wonder we are witnessing a global moral meltdown as the rise of religious fundamentalism wars with an increasingly pervasive technology. We have lived so long in this two-truth universe that we may figure it was always this way. It wasn't.

Throughout most of history, people's work world and spiritual worlds interacted. When the enslaved Hebrews of Egypt, the down-trodden slaves of imperial Rome, the dispossessed widows and orphans of seventh-century Arabia, and the "untouchables" of Siddhartha's India were suffering in mind and body, they evolved a spiritual response appropriate for their time and circumstances. And from those experiences came a body of literature written between 1300 B.C. and A.D. 650: the Bible, the Koran, the Vedas, the Gita, the Tao te Ching, and the teachings of Confucius and Buddha.

To a world that was flat, static, agricultural, and largely illiterate, those books were, literally, a godsend. They served their times exceptionally well. Unfortunately, the core teachings were set in cultural contexts that have been largely superseded. The religious traditions of antiquity are hard pressed now to guide us in a brave new world that was never foreseen by their authors.

With the atom smasher, the gene machine, the digital computer, psychoactive drugs, we manipulate matter, life, mind, and mood today in a way we thought only God could do fifty years ago. Yet we attempt to exercise these abilities in a "value-free" context, with no generally accepted moral code appropriate for our new power. Who is to teach us? I have not found one school of divinity that offers courses in science and technology as part of the core curriculum, yet every religion recognizes that *"God is manifest through nature."*

Reflecting on the lack of spirituality appropriate to our time, and the hunger for such, is the popularity today of medieval plainchant and Renaissance angels (a flight to the past), or a loopy New Ageism that lacks any rigor, discipline, or spine, holding that all values are of equal value, and hence, of no value.

Until such time as the leaders of the world's religious traditions can transcend their cultural and dogmatic differences, it falls to individuals and communities of like-minded people to evolve a spirituality appropriate for our time. This isn't heresy.

Every great religion originally appeared as a response among people desperate for comfort and solace during troubled times. And the irony is that in this exercise today we can actually combine what we know about science with our need to get closer to our spiritual core.

Science and technology deal with things: atoms and galaxies, levers and microprocessors. The life of the spirit, on the other hand, deals with connections between things; mercy, justice, and love. We have become very good in the age of science and technology at knowing about things, but we're not really as wise as we should be at making the connections.

The great naturalist John Muir once said, "I find that if I touch anything, it's connected to everything else in the universe." True spirituality is an exquisite awareness of the interconnection of all things. And the connection of connections, the network of networks, the bond of all bonds is the phenomenon we call God, an old English word meaning "the good."

Instead of picturing God as a medieval monarch on a marble throne, imagine God as the living awareness in the space between the atoms, "empty" space that makes up 99.9 percent of the universe. Thinking of God that way gets us past some of the great theological divides of the past. Is God imminent or transcendent, internal or external, composed or compassionate? Like the question of whether the atom is a wave or particle, the answer is: yes.

Rituals and formulas aside, prayer is the act of simplicity itself. Batteries are not required and there's no heavy lifting. Afterward, you can still drive and operate heavy machinery. When we pray, it's not so important how we bend our knees or fold our arms. The life of the spirit has less to do with the angularity of our limbs and more to do with the straightness of our hearts.

Electronic engineers concern themselves with what they call a signal-to-noise ratio. They want to engineer products that put out a strong signal with minimal interference. You can hear this phenomenon on the radio. We'd all be well-advised to put aside a certain time each day, or certainly each week, to pause and reflect on the signals of meaning in our lives. This discerning is probably the root idea of the Sabbath, spending one-seventh of the week reflecting on the signal of life's meaning apart from the noise of distraction.

The seventeenth century gave us the Scientific Revolution. The nineteenth century spawned the Industrial Revolution. So perhaps the twenty-first century will give us a Spiritual Revolution to tie it all together. But only if each of us—individually and collectively—makes it so.

Light, Love, Action, and a Camera

On November 20, 1995 (my birthday), I was with a friend on a tour of the New Conservatory Theater Center in San Francisco. In passing we were introduced to Lois Tema, a photographer whose studio was located in the building. Following an immediate and strong knowing that I wanted to schedule a photo shoot with her, I asked for her card. I said I would call to schedule an appointment. I felt a visceral knowing that she was the one who was *supposed* to do the photograph for the jacket of this book. There was not a single doubt in my mind that this was so.

Upon leaving the premises, my friend questioned me, asking why I'd said I was going to do that when I'd never even seen a portfolio of her work. Knowing there was no way to explain it, I just reaffirmed my belief that I somehow knew I wanted her to take the picture.

A month later, at a business meeting, I requested a check to pay for the photo shoot even though I had not yet scheduled it. I passed Lois's business card to Doug Hackett, secretary-treasurer of Entagram Productions Inc., so he could make a check payable to her. When he found out that I had not seen her work or set up a time to see it, he and others suggested leaving the payee blank, in case I changed my mind after seeing her portfolio. "Please make it payable to Lois Tema."

At the end of December I called to schedule the session. Not surprisingly, Lois did not remember our meeting. It was a challenge to coordinate our schedules, as she was getting ready to go on pregnancy leave and I was in town only until January 12. The first and only time she had available was January 11 at 11 A.M! I wrote it down and laughed. "1-11, 11:00 A.M." It looked right to me!

In the following two weeks, every kind of physical and emotional upset that could possibly happen in one's life seemed to occur in mine. On top of that I got a classic case of the flu. Two days before the photo shoot, I was seriously sleep deprived, only a day or so past the flu, and suffering terribly from what was, in spite of surgery, a chronic toothache. As you might imagine, this did not bode well for having a decent photo taken.

That evening, when Lois called to confirm our appointment, my friend spoke with her. She told her what I'd been through and said she didn't know if I was going to be able to keep the engagement. Lois asked her to have me call that night if I was going to have to cancel; otherwise she would have to be paid, regardless.

When I returned, I considered the options—and looked in the mirror. I knew in spite of what I saw that I had to go. I'd have to pray that makeup could cover the lack of sleep and the ravages of the flu, and called to confirm I'd be there at the appointed hour.

I arrived the following morning, and as I was doing my hair and makeup, Lois went about setting up the shoot. During this time, we began to talk about the pending arrival of her first child—she was eight and a half months pregnant—and about life in general.

When she asked me the obvious question about my book, I replied with my standard answer—never knowing where people are coming from—"It's called *The Pattern*, and it's an inspirational book about the origin of the Pattern. The Pattern may also be a form that embraces truths in all religions, and in modern science as well."

This definitely got her attention. She began to ask me if I knew "so and so," which I didn't, and shared with me that she was part of a group who had been exploring spiritual truths together every Friday for ten years. She casually asked if I had any understanding of Buddhism—not that she was Buddhist—at which time I told her that His Holiness the Dalai Lama had been presented with the first three-dimensional model of the Pattern.

Hearing this, Lois got an incredulous but knowing look on her face. "Lynnclaire," she asked, "by any chance does your book have anything to do with a symbol carved on a large black stone at a temple somewhere in Hawai'i?"

Now, I thought I was inured to cosmic coincidence, but once again the Divine Master Mischief Maker got to say, "Gotcha!"

I looked at Lois and replied, "That's my stone. That's the Pattern."

She told me that as soon as I told her the title of the book, the stone flashed in her mind, and she knew it had to be the same. And then she told me the rest of the story.

A year previously, Lois and her husband had gone to Hawai'i on their honeymoon. While there, a dear friend from O'ahu took them to the Big Island to see the volcano and to visit the nearby Nechung Dorje Drayang Ling temple. Lois and her friend were descending the stone steps that led to the back side of the Tara temple when she said they felt an inexplicable rush of energy. Almost immediately they saw the large lava stone sitting at the base of the steps. She went on to tell me that they sat down next to it and for at least half an hour contemplated the symbol engraved in the stone. She said she knew it was important and tried to draw it, but couldn't. She felt further thwarted as they didn't have a camera.

Her experience was sounding very, very familiar.

She also laughingly admitted that so powerful was her connection to that sixty-to-seventy-pound stone that if she'd had any less character she would have attempted to pilfer it!

We were both laughing with amazement, but she wasn't finished with her story. Several times in the past year, she had asked this friend to please get her a photo of the stone the next time he was on the Big Island. What's more, less than a week ago, this friend called and left a message saying he was coming to the mainland in a couple of weeks and would love to see Lois and her husband when he passed through San Francisco.

Lois immediately returned his call, telling him they'd love to see him, but more than that, she'd really love it if he showed up with the picture of the symbol. She told him if he didn't already have it, would he please go to the Big Island before he came and take the picture.

We were laughing and both near tears when she looked at me and said, "Lynnclaire, as soon as you said the name of your book, I knew that symbol had to be the pattern you were talking about."

Now, I have to tell you, we took a *lot* of pictures that day, and we both knew that every one would turn out, simply because every smile was so heart-fully genuine! What normally would have been an hour session wound up being almost three.

This episode provided me with many lessons in consciousness. Again, I realized what amazing grace and gifts are presented to us when we honor our intuitive knowing—especially when we are given numerous opportunities to discount it. I also saw, through Lois's steadfast intention and repeated requests, how the Divine delivers answers to our requests. She certainly received a positive R.S.V.P. to her invitation to have the Pattern come into her life.

And then, suddenly, I had yet another knowing.

"Lois, when *exactly* were you on the Big Island?" I asked.

"Let me get my calendar. I can tell you precisely the day we were there."

"We would have been there on Sunday, January 15."

I knew it. Lois saw the Pattern for the first time *exactly* seven years to the day after I saw it for the first time.

Coincidence? I think not.

More to be revealed? I think so!

C H A P T E R   T W E L V E

China: The Rooster Crows

Paper Walls

*A*n invitation to join my dear friend Steve Bryson on a trip to China in July 1996 culminated in a magical journey. It was one of the more wondrous, nonlogical episodes that have comprised my life for the past nine years.

Both Steve and I intuitively knew there was a Grand Plan in operation. I believed that it was somehow connected to the Circle of Elders I have been getting to "know" in my meditations for the past four years. One night, as Steve and I were talking, I told him of the Asian man who was part of this circle. I had seen this man so many times in my dreams that in late 1991 I sculpted his image in red clay. A further meditative experience in early 1992, with my friend Lael, led me to believe that this man might show up in "real" time wearing a blue-and-white-striped shirt. Steve and I speculated whether we might encounter this man, one I knew only as a "healer," on our trip.

Even though we suspected that, in addition to being a cultural adventure, this journey might have something to do with the Pattern, we determined to remain quiet on the subject unless we had clear direction otherwise. Sensitive to the political environment and uncertain as to how our message might be received, we did not want to say or do anything that might jeopardize our visit. I determined to live the Pattern, not talk about it.

On the fourth of July we departed Hong Kong, making the short flight to Guangzhou (formerly Canton) in southern China, where we cleared Chinese immigration. Our arrival at the airport was truly an experience of "close encounters"—personal space was virtually nonexistent, and I discovered in a new way what it meant to be part of a collective consciousness. I found very quickly that my "safe space" was nowhere save within my own consciousness.

In the midsummer monsoon, one feels a particular density to China as one moves slowly in the vast throngs of people. The air was ripe with foreign smells and filled with vibrant yet cacophonous sound. The roads teemed with pedestrians, bicycles, and carts pulled by man or mule, and when we boarded one of the many varieties of buses we felt "vacuum-packed."

At every turn I was met with unfamiliar sounds and incredible sights. The somatic realities of China's culture were mind boggling. My travels in Europe and South America had done nothing to prepare me for Asia. Even the brief overnight layover in Hong Kong failed to prime me, for there everything is geared toward Western sensitivities.

Within moments of clearing immigration I was immersed in a world unlike any I had ever known. Around us the volume of life was cranked to the max, and curiosity and vigilance met us at every turn. Yet, only two things were required to transform this watchfulness into enthusiastic embrace: (1) a genuine, heartfelt smile and (2) the words (spelled phonetically) "nee-how" and "she-she" (as in shed, without the "d"), the basic equivalents to "hello" and "thank you" in Mandarin. As Steve put it, the walls separating us as human beings were not insurmountable or made of stone; rather they were paper thin.

I soon realized that Western standards of cleanliness are not universal. But as we were repeatedly touched by the pure and generous hearts of the Chinese, I became aware that surface cleanliness has nothing whatsoever to do with godliness. The love and generosity of spirit I experienced quickly broke down my personal and culturally transmitted sensibilities, and I saw them for what they really are—sociological bigotry. As never before I saw that what I take as "rights" are nothing if not privilege.

Flexibility and acceptance became my watchwords. I had been in China only a few hours when I concluded that if unconditional love means unconditional acceptance, then I must reject any personal value whose foundation was only tolerance.

I learned both how resilient and how fixed I am when I was presented with a hole in the ground for a toilet. No door, no semblance of privacy. In addition, no one had remembered to tell me toilet paper was something you must supply yourself. I couldn't help but realize that we—the global human family—are truly approaching a crossroads.

Once we arrived in Nanjing, a city with few Western visitors (especially in the middle of the monsoon season), I felt as though we were at the center of a compass, two diametrical worlds converging. Nanjing is an inland coastal industrial city—actually a village of more than four million—approximately six hundred miles south-southeast of Beijing.

Here, we were guests in the home of our most gracious hostess, who had extended an invitation to Steve the year before when he met her son, Michael, a computer scientist, and Joy, his fiancée, at a conference in Beijing. Almost immediately we felt a mutual sense of "family" and discovered that it came from our shared sense of spirituality.

The second day we were there, Michael and Joy began to share their backgrounds with us. We were fascinated to learn that Michael's late father had been a top government official in Nanjing. His responsibilities following the cultural revolution included the restoration of many of Nanjing's religious sites, and he was also instrumental in the release of cultural prisoners.

Late that night, after hearing their fascinating stories, they asked about my book. Cautiously I set aside my initial intuitive hesitation and showed the Pattern to Michael and Joy. I also told them about the Asian man in my vision.

Of Dreams and Daydreams: Where Concurrent Realities Merge

The following morning Michael arranged for us to spend a few hours with a dear friend of his father, Liú Dà Rèn, secretary-general of the Buddhist Association in Nanjing. We met at Jï Mín Temple, one of China's oldest Buddhist monastic temples. Michael told us that he and Joy would act as our translators, as Teacher Liú spoke no English.

As soon as we were escorted to the small patio and introductions were made, Steve and I checked in with one another. We were both amazed, as this was, without a doubt, the man whose face I had sculpted five years before. And he was wearing a blue-and-white-striped shirt! We sat hand in hand as Michael, Joy, and Teacher Liú spoke in Chinese, only later learning that this was their first reunion since Michael's father's death.

What's more, this was the first time Teacher Liú had met Joy. We later learned the depth of his heart connection to Michael, as Michael's father was responsible for placing Teacher Liú in a position that would allow him to ascend to his current position.

As often as possible, Joy would stop the dialogue and translate for us. Soon we left the office to take a tour of the temple, realizing anew the miracle unfolding as a result of Michael's father's vision. The preeminent architectural restoration was the reconstruction of the tower located at the heart of the grounds, a structure that ascended seven stories. When we entered the first level, I was delighted to discover a huge Healing Medicine Buddha. As Joy translated, I shared my personal connection with this particular emanation of the Buddha. I told Teacher Liú that one of my most important advisors in America is a practitioner in the Medicine Buddha tradition. Teacher Liú then took me by the hand, telling me that on each of the seven levels was yet another expression of this same Buddha. Together we climbed higher and higher. As we stood together at the top, looking out over the city, the four of us expressed our gratitude and appreciation for Liú Dà Rèn's life, knowing that our meeting was another simple demonstration of grace and divine order.

That morning we were given a tour of the temple's inner sites, locations seldom seen by the Chinese, and rarely if ever by foreigners. We viewed the rare rainbow-colored remains of a revered abbess and saw her single wooden prayer bead that would not burn when she was cremated. We were allowed to observe and photograph Buddhas under construction, as artisans and their apprentices demonstrated their centuries-old craftsmanship. We watched them work in clay, stone, and wood, and paint intricate patterns they had practiced by drawing in the dust. I was allowed to hold the hand of a small Buddha sculpture before it was put into place and then fired in the kiln.

Before we returned to Teacher Liú's patio for refreshments, Steve and I both purchased Kuan Yin sculptures, his a magnificent work in bronze, mine in wood. Liú Dà Rèn asked us to leave them there so that he could arrange for them to be blessed. We knew this was another wonderful gift.

When we were seated, Teacher Liú excused himself for a moment and disappeared into his office. At this time Michael and Joy told me that I must show him the Pattern and share my story. They had said nothing about me except that I was a writer.

When he returned we were all surprised when he handed me a painting he had obviously just completed. He asked Joy to translate as he explained this still-damp watercolor of a man sitting—floating—in a ring of circles that appeared to be a tunnel or perhaps a cave. This was the man, he said, who fifteen hundred years ago came from India, bringing the message of Chan Buddhism to China. The man (known in India as Bodhidharma) had spent nine years meditating in a cave before his journey. Teacher Liú surprised all of us when he expressed his feeling that I had a connection with this man. I was in tears and speechless.

He then told us he had made special arrangements for us to leave immediately for another part of the city where we would visit China's resurrected Buddhist Printing Company and China's official Office for Buddhist Studies. This was a place seldom visited by foreigners.

There we saw dozens of huge hand-carved stones that are still used to create magnificent works of art, and tens of thousands of hand-cut wooden blocks that had been preserved and were once again being used to print ancient Buddhist texts. We saw the simple tables where artisans hand color this work and the crowded room where workers collate one page at a time and bind each volume by hand.

Later that evening we were guests in the home of Teacher Liú and his gracious wife. One of the most memorable moments of the trip was when he took us to his altar and brought out a picture of Michael's father, which he keeps in a special place there.

It was quite late that night when I finally told him the story of the Pattern. His face lit up as I finished the "short version" of the story and completed my simple drawings of the Pattern's many perspectives. As soon as I finished, he began to speak. He had so much to say that Joy had a hard time keeping up!

That night he told us that the world needed and was ready for the message of the Pattern. He reminded us that China held one-quarter of the world's population. He offered to assist in cultural translation and editing, helping in any way he could to get the Pattern and its message to China's people.

Shortly after, we learned two things that held great meaning for me. One was that the name of the Nanjing temple, Jī Mín, translates as "the rooster crows," the place that issues a wake-up call to the people. The second was that, soon after returning from nineteen years of manual labor in the countryside to atone for his upper-class background, Teacher Liú changed his given name to Dà Rèn—meaning "the man with the big task."

The morning of July 11, two cars from the Buddhist Association were sent to pick us up and escort us to a monastery and temple about an hour outside the city. This particular temple, Qi Xia, is now considered one of China's cultural treasures. We were awed by the alignment of natural beauty and structural form. Unlike Jī Mín Temple, at Qi Xia Temple most of the one thousand Buddhas sculpted in rocks on the beautiful mountain behind the temple were not damaged during the cultural revolution. Rather, they were destroyed by war a century ago at the end of the Qing dynasty. During the cultural revolution, troops were housed in Qi Xia Temple, and their tenancy is the main reason it survived.

The five of us shared many memories, thoughts, hopes, dreams, and visions on the mountain that day. Over lunch, Teacher Liú asked me to tell the story of our connection in my book. He asked me to tell those in the West about the spiritual awakening that is happening all across China. As we shared from the heart, we all realized that although our personalities, egos, dreams, and desires had been and continue to be refined by the fire of life, healing was and always is possible. We all agreed that the highest intention of our souls had quite wondrously delivered us to this place and time.

After visiting yet another temple, where we met an inspiring eighty-two-year-old monk who has lived through the many changes in China, we returned to Jï Mín Temple for the blessing of the Kuan Yin sculptures.

As soon as we entered and began to make the long, hot ascent to the top of the temple grounds, I became aware of a dramatic shift in the energy from two days before. I soon realized that this was the effect of the chanting that echoed over the entire area.

That day, one of China's most esteemed Buddhist priests was at Jï Mín Temple. At that moment he was leading more than one hundred nuns, a handful of monks, and a large group of Chinese in a ceremony to honor the anniversary of the death of the last director of Jï Mín, the revered abbess with rainbow-colored remains we had seen earlier.

When the dedication ceremony concluded, I was approached by two young women. They introduced themselves by their Western names, Fay and Sherry, and told me they were students at Nanjing University. Fay pointedly asked me, "Do you really believe in this?" indicating the external demonstration of life's spiritual dimension. I took her hand and told her, "Yes, I do, because it's true."

When she then asked a penetrating "Why?" all I could do was respond from the heart, telling her, "We aren't physical beings here on Earth trying to find God through religious or mental experiences. We're spiritual beings here to remember who and what we are, and we do this through our physical life—a life that is composed of mental and emotional experiences." I went on as quickly as I could, telling her, "In my heart and mind and body—my whole life—I believe that this is how we know and make love real. It's true, Fay. Love is what this life experience is all about."

Then she said, "I've studied Hinduism and other religions, and, to me, they all seem to be the same. But because they all fight with one another, and try to change each other, and no one accepts the other, I'm not sure I can believe that love comes out of any of it."

Before we could complete any further thoughts, the nun I had met earlier appeared and asked me to join Michael, Steve, and Teacher Liú at the main temple. Here we were introduced to the Buddhist priest.

We joined the crowd that had gathered inside the temple around the main altar. Both of us were surprised when we were led to the kneeling benches right behind the priest, and Teacher Liú indicated that we were to follow the priest in the service. We were enclosed within a three-sided pyramid, each side formed by eight monks and nuns. Surrounded by this energy, we knew this was going to be much more than the simple blessing of two pieces of sacred art.

We followed the priest through seven prostrations, followed by prayers and chants. It was indicated that I should go to the altar and gather and light small bundles of incense. When I returned we did three more prostrations, after which this revered priest picked up a small bowl of water from the altar and three times went around the circle sprinkling it on both the altar—including our Kuan Yin sculptures—and everyone in the audience.

Following more prostrations and prayers, he picked up a small hand mirror and began to shine it throughout the room. I somehow knew that he was using this small round mirror—its shape reflecting the feminine, the moon, and the earth—to gather light and energy from the altar and the individuals present. I was surprised once again when he brought the mirror and held it up to my face. I knew I was meant not to look at myself, but to look inward. He then handed me the mirror and returned to the altar, where he concluded the blessing.

Suddenly I found myself surrounded by those who had been in the audience. As they bowed and thanked me I was embarrassed, since I had done absolutely nothing. I searched my mind to find some experience that was analogous to what I was feeling—the closest was that of being a bride at a wedding reception. In that moment all I could do was embrace and thank them, honoring them for allowing me to be there and have this profound experience.

Fay and her friend Sherry were the last ones waiting, and Fay's simple words to me were the crowning of the day: "What I have seen has opened my heart. I believe." Sherry told me that the day before was her nineteenth birthday, but that today she had received her present.

Moments later in Teacher Liú's office we learned the significance of what had occurred. It was only because the priest happened to be present and because we were good friends of Líu Dà Rèn's, as well as Westerners who admired Buddhism deeply, that the priest was permitted to perform this particular blessing, considered most auspicious by the Chinese Buddhists. It was, in fact, a Kuan Yin initiation, an empowerment service of such serious nature held by such a high monk that most Chinese people can rarely afford the expense of this blessing ceremony. However, because I literally had touched the heart of each person I thanked, I had—unknowingly—passed on to them this gift I had received.

The small red hand mirror now sits on my altar with my Kuan Yin sculpture. I feel graced to hold this small piece of glass that, for me, reflects the light that emanates from deep within the heart of China and its people.

CHAPTER THIRTEEN

In Closing, a New Beginning

A Caveat

*I*n this introduction to the Pattern, I realize that you have seen it through a series of progressive lenses that I have worn along the way. My experience and teachers periodically ground me new lenses when things began to move out of focus.

My soul's intention is that my words be extensions of essential Love. It is my hope that the Pattern will evoke a collaborative heart response from you, and that you will accept its invitation to join with me and others in the joyous Dance of Life.

I honor the fact that the Pattern will elicit many responses and have a different meaning to every person, according to each one's personal values, beliefs, and life experience.

There may be those who will want to use the Pattern for artistic purposes—painters, writers, sculptors, or weavers. If the simplicity of its beauty inspires someone to create a passionate expression of loving compassion, it will have facilitated healing.

Devout believers of many faiths have said that the Pattern reflects their truth and contains their sacred symbols. The Pattern supports all faiths and all people's God-given right to lovingly express their tradition. This work seeks only to encourage all in exercising the Love that is the core of their beliefs. It does not seek to change them.

As the Pattern illumines our common genesis it will reveal new depths of who and what we are—spiritual beings having an earthly experience.

Others are already studying the Pattern as it relates to particular scientific disciplines.

There are those in the healing professions—both traditional and alternative—who have expressed a desire to explore the Pattern's psycho-physiological impact, knowing that since time immemorial, symbols have been powerful tools in healing.

Some see the Pattern as a means for joining diverse groups in a common cause of universal truth—Love. Imagine what this world would be if we established relationship on a single foundation of integrity, honoring our uniqueness while celebrating our sameness with unconditional love and acceptance.

Some philosophers, psychologists, and theologians may have a field day with the Pattern. Doubtless it will spark debates. I pray that through such discourse this three-dimensional world will become aligned with higher-dimensional worlds.

Heart response to the Pattern may challenge mental assumptions. Although it may prompt inner deliberation, it does not require the renunciation or acceptance of a particular religion, creed, or doctrine. The Pattern deconstructs the old paradigm of "us or them," "winner or loser." It merely calls forth the remembrance of Love.

Those of a metaphysical inclination may see the Pattern as an expression of another reality.

There are those who already want to create temples and organize a new church around the Pattern. This is not my job, nor is it the intention of the Pattern. You are the temple! Find a space where you feel safe to evolve and grow. Embrace the divinity within your being and join with people of like mind and heart and express love with compassion.

Then there are some who see the Pattern as an entity, an otherworldly, celestial form presenting itself among us, a "crop circle" being impressed upon human consciousness. Others have called it the grail. It is not for me to say. I pray only that the Pattern will give rise to a dialogue of peace and that pieces of it will be cosmic, karmic, and comic! We all need to laugh more!

Yes, global dialogues may probe the historical, mythological, mystical, and archetypal images represented in the Pattern. There may be lengthy discourses on its influence. However, remember this one truth, a truth that I believe without hesitation—the Pattern is here now, in this reality, to bring heavenly minded matters down to earth for earthly good.

Three weeks following my first near-death experience, I experienced my second near-death episode, and this time I was presented with the opportunity to *choose* life or death. As you have read in the preceding pages, I chose life and returned with the Pattern. I believe that I returned for the children—pure beings of Love who come into this world without reluctance and in many cases with no welcoming committee to greet them.

Not surprisingly, it is the children who see the Pattern and proclaim, "I remember that! It's in my heart!"

It is the child—the child within and the child without—who immediately knows that all the perspectives of the Pattern are the same.

It is the children who sit down with a box of color crayons and draw this simple form without giving its complexity a second thought.

The children are the ones who see the Pattern and jump up, hold hands with their friends, twirl in circles, laugh, and call out, "Look, Lynnclaire! We're dancing the Pattern!" And like one five-year-old bundle of joy who recently sat next to me as I explained "the story" to her older siblings said, "I know, it's all about love."

How we love the children—the children of the world and the inner children who are ourselves—is the heart of the matter. This love we share is all that matters in the face of eternity. How we choose to color the future for our children and our children's children will be the lasting legacy we leave when we depart this earth. Love is the only cure that will heal the ailing hearts of the children and the planet.

Remember that as we mix our tears with Light, we, children all, color the world with a rainbow of Love.

MAY WE ALL BE CATALYSTS,

one spark among many,

FOR CHANGE,

the transition from one to the transformation of Oneness,

FOR LOVE,

cherishing all life and having compassion for all beings.

MAY WE BRING FORTH,

willing to lead others through the shadows of doubt and despair
into the full light of forgiveness,

HOLD,

to nurture, embrace, and protect,

AND HONOR,

to restore dignity to the soul,

REMEMBRANCE,

the ember of memory that still glows and recalls the genesis
of all existence.

MAY WE BRING TO CONSCIOUS
AWARENESS,

assisting others out of the abyss of fear and placing them upon a new
foundation of peace,

THE REALMS,

the unlimited expanse of the universe and Love,

THE REALITIES,

the infinite coexistence and concurrent truths of time and space
throughout the seasons, cycles, and circles of life,

AND THE REMNANTS,

*the mental shreds and tattered emotional remains of our Goddessential
being that become the seeds to the restoration of our bodies, minds,
souls, and our earthly home,*

IN ORDER,

*following the divine matrix of Oneness for the continuation of the
fulfillment of a Divine Plan that is essential for the integration and
atonement of all sentient beings,*

THAT THE SPIRIT,

*the blithe and childlike piece of ourselves who is continually awed by the
magic of the sunset and enchanted by the beauty of a rose,*

MAY

*without reservation, governed only by self-determination and guided by
heartfelt intention,*

REMEMBER

to every moment recall and rejoin

THE DANCE,

*the collective influence that arises out of the harmony that inspires
humanity and can move mountains,
where illusion dissolves and love becomes real as a commitment is made,
where humankind and the Divine Hand that set the universe in motion
agree to cooperate in the work of regeneration.*

MAY LOVE BE SO.

ACKNOWLEDGMENTS

With Wonder, Awe, and Gratitude

*I*t is impossible to list the names of all who have held the light for both my presence and this work. You know who you are, and your names are inscribed upon the tablet of my heart. I thank you from the depth of my being. You are my teachers and I am honored to call you my friends.

To my friends and spiritual "family" at EPI, no words can adequately express my gratitude.

And Stewart and Tish, there simply are not enough words . . . you are loved.

My love, respect, awe, and appreciation to my three closest buddies: my mom, Joyce Dennis Knudson, a.k.a. Spunky, the quintessential mother who loved the "me" before January 15, 1987, and loves me still;

Danny O'Connor, the brother of my heart who for seven long years, countless lifetimes, and Goddessence only knows how many incarnations in this one body has been there to sustain my soul, and when I forget is there to remind me who I really am;

And my closest confidant, Lael Montgomery, who has redefined sisterhood.

—**Lynnclaire**

183

𝒯he 𝒫attern 𝒞ollection ™

THE PATTERN PIN

Actual size approximately 1 1/4"; the center sphere will be faceted.

This stunning replica of the Pattern's primary perspective, *The Heart of Intimacy*, has been designed and created by award-winning jeweler Douglas Koorey exclusively for **The Pattern Collection™**. Celebrate all creation's Goddessential Oneness by wearing this radiant expression of love, peace, and unity. Designed with a tie-tack back, it can be worn as a lapel pin by both men and women. Or suspend it from your favorite chain and wear it as a pendant.

This unique, handcrafted keepsake is available in solid sterling silver for $89.95, or in fashion gold plate for $39.95, plus shipping and handling.

THE PATTERN VIDEO
𝒜 𝒱isual 𝒨editational 𝓔xperience
20 minutes, $19.95, plus shipping and handling

Executive producer: Lynnclaire Dennis

Produced and animated by Wiseguys' Graphics, Seattle, Washington

Music: "The Music of Genesis," © 1992 by Stephen James Taylor, BMI; Kiba Dachi Music, BMI, publisher; and Stan Tenen (for the Meru Foundation). Original concept by Stan Tenen for the Meru Foundation.

See all of the Pattern's intricate and multidimensional aspects in this truly inspirational video! Be among the first to visually explore the Pattern, viewing this complex and dynamic structure both inside and out. Journey through the Pattern to sacred sites around the world, and venture into the farthest reaches of the known universe. Witness the Pattern as a mirror of Nature's own patterns, its beauty reflected in all living systems. Be profoundly moved by the hauntingly familiar melody "The Music of Genesis," a mathematical interpretation of the pattern found in the ancient Hebrew letters comprising the first verse of Genesis, the first book of the Bible. This music is the incredible conceptual result of twenty-five years of research into the Kabbalah by Stan Tenen.

Because scientists have not yet been able to write a mathematical formula from which the Pattern can be computer-generated, hundreds of hours of meticulous, manual animation were required to produce this spectacular video.

Your heart and your mind will open as you appreciate in a new way the Wonder of Oneness—all sentient beings' Goddessential connection. Truly a holistic sensory experience!

THE PATTERN SCREEN SAVER

$12.95, plus shipping and handling

Please specify Mac or PC version.

To place your order, call THE PATTERN:
1-800-575-1612

Please allow 4 to 6 weeks for delivery.

THE PATTERN WORLD WIDE WEB SITE

http://www.kitsap.net/pattern/